EVERY
FOLLOWER
A
LEADER
And
EVERY LEADER A FOLLOWER

WES NEAL

CROSS TRAINING
PUBLISHING

Every Follower A Leader

Wes Neal, Every Follower A Leader

ISBN 1-929478-86-0

Cross Training Publishing
P.O. Box 1874
Kearney, NE 68848
(308) 293-3891

www.crosstrainingpublishing.com

Copyright © 2006 by Wes Neal

This book is manufactured in the
United States of America.

CONTENTS

GETTING STARTED

ON THE ROAD WITH JESUS

EXTRAS

CONTACT INFORMATION

AUTHOR E-MAILS

Wesnealcoe@aol.com

wes@wesneal.com

AUTHOR WEBSITES

Total Release Sports

www.totalreleasesports.com

15 Days of God

www.15daysofgod.com

Wes Neal Resources

www.wesnealresources.com

CROSS TRAINING PUBLISHING

www.crosstrainingpublishing.com

P.O. Box 1874, Kearney, NE 68848

308-293-3891

To My Six Grandkids

McKenzie, Molly and Cole Duncan,
and
Tommy, Ella, and Abigail Anthony

**The "funnest," "bestest," and
greatest kids in the world!**

Each one of you, in your own way, lights up the world around you. I know you light up my world. I love that in each of you now, and I can't wait to see how that will continue as you grow older.

Let me tell you something. What your "Pops" wants the most is for each of you to choose to follow Jesus, and be caught up in His special plan for you in building God's Kingdom. He has a crystal-clear role for you to play, you know.

As you do that, you'll be the Follower-Leader God has uniquely designed you to be. No one else just like you. And, do you know what? People you meet, along the way, will have the highest opinion of you. Both Jesus and I already do. Oh, by the way, just in case you're wondering. Each of you is my favorite.

DEDICATION OF SECTIONS

Many highways you travel on have sections of the road dedicated to different people, or organizations. The "highway," winding through this book does, too. You'll find these dedications, along with why that particular section of the book is dedicated, on the back of each introductory sheet. Like the one opposite this page.

GETTING STARTED

DEDICATED TO
THE "TRIPLE THREAT"

This section is in honor of the people on staff with Athletes in Action, the athletic arm of Campus Crusade for Christ, as well as all of CCC; the Fellowship of Christian Athletes; and, Kanakuk Kamps. Each of these great organizations help people "get started" on their journey with God, and help them along the way become effective Follower-Leaders. This section will help you "get started" on your "on the road" adventure with Jesus.

ABOUT THE BOOK

Arrangement of the "On the Road" Episodes

Many "harmonies" have been written on the life and teachings of Jesus. Works that mesh all four biblical accounts of Jesus' life together. However, the one I have long used is the LIFE OF CHRIST IN STEREO, by Johnston Cheney. Mr. Cheney, a Greek scholar, first carefully scrutinized the Greek manuscripts of all four biographies of Jesus in the Bible. Then, he meshed each of the accounts into one, keeping everything in each of the four biographies, except duplications.

As you read EVERY FOLLOWER A LEADER, you'll notice a Bible reference under each page title. References that go from one Bible account to another. Although we do go from Matthew to John, back to Matthew, then onto Mark and Luke, etc., it is done in the chronological order of Jesus' life, according to LIFE OF CHRIST IN STEREO.

Four-Year Outreach

You'll also notice I used a four-year approach to Jesus' outreach. That's also based on Mr. Cheney's findings from the Bible. There are several reasons for this, two of which I'll mention here.

First, there are just too many events in the last year of the traditional three-year approach to Jesus' ministry for them to all have happened in one year. It makes more sense to divide that last stretch into two years.

Second, the parable Jesus told in Luke 13:6-9 has definite overtones to His own ministry. He tells of the owner of a vineyard who has been waiting for three years for a fig tree to produce any fruit. Then, after wanting to cut it down, the man who tends the vineyard talked the owner into giving it one more year to produce. The owner agreed.

Now, if this is a parable that parallels Jesus own ministry, which many Bible scholars believe it is, then Jesus had a four-year ministry.

So, what difference does it make? Three year, or four year. Absolutely none. No matter how long Jesus' ministry was, all of His important teachings and events are included in the Bible. The only reason I'm letting you know, in advance of your reading, is so you won't be caught by surprise at the four-year approach I'm taking.

Pronoun Usage

Throughout the book, I'm using a masculine pronoun, such as *he, his, him,* whenever the gender doesn't matter. I've done that just for simplicity. For example, it reads easier to say, "when someone approaches you, and *he* asks…" than to say, "when someone approaches you, and *he or she* asks…"

Well, you get the idea.

4

Color Commentary

Most of my writing is based on what the biblical account reveals, as well as the culture of Jesus' day. However, I will also include some of my own speculative thoughts. Simply to add a little mental imagery, or color commentary, to the teaching, or episode.

Whenever you read the words, "perhaps," "most likely," "probably," "might have," etc, those introduce my color comments. My purpose is to fill in how it "most likely" happened. Not to add something that "probably" wasn't there.

Age of Jesus

Finally, concerning the age of Jesus. Again, like the year span of His outreach, His age is not very important. However, for the sake of accuracy, in "His Time Had Come," on page 21, I wrote: "When Jesus was in His early thirties…" That phrase introduces Him coming to be baptized.

It is traditionally thought that Jesus started His mission at thirty years of age, and that He was crucified when He was no older than thirty-four, based on a three-year span. Now, if we look at the actual biblical record, and not tradition, we'll see that Jesus was in His early thirties when He started out. That would make Him about thirty-six or thirty-seven when He was crucified, if we use a four-year span.

How do we arrive at that? The only biblical reference to Jesus' adult age is in Luke 3:23, "Jesus was about thirty years old when He began his public ministry." Interestingly, Luke was known for his precise writing. He was a master of details. Yet, in mentioning Jesus' age, Luke didn't write that Jesus WAS thirty years of age. Only that he was ABOUT thirty. That's another way to say, He was either in His early thirties, or in His late twenties.

Because Luke gave exact details in other places of his narrative, if Jesus were actually thirty years old, Luke would have written that, "Jesus WAS thirty years old..." He didn't. He only gave an approximate age.

We can also look at other people Luke mentioned concerning the birth of Jesus. He mentioned King Herod in Luke 1:5, the Roman emperor, Caesar Augustus, in Luke 2:1, and the Syrian governor, Quirinius, in Luke 2:2. Because we know the exact dates of those people mentioned, and because we know when John the Baptist went public, we can assume that Jesus was in His early thirties.

Again, not that it really matters.

THE GREATEST LEADER

For the last several years, I have gleaned tips from some of the best sport coaches, as well as business people, in the land. As much as I appreciate, and pass on to others, what I have learned from them, I have yet to find anyone who even comes close to the leadership skills I've learned from Jesus, the man from Galilee.

Has there ever been anyone who can measure up to the lasting world influence this one carpenter from an insignificant spot in the world has had? Notice I said "lasting." Not just for a decade, or even a hundred years. But, down through the centuries.

Oh, you might say, Moses wasn't too shabby. And, then there was Mohammad. Two great and powerful leaders. Yet, compare them side to side with Jesus, teaching for teaching, method for method, results for results. From my observation, and even the observation of Jesus' enemies, none match up to Jesus by comparing all three criteria.

Jesus not only stands alone as a leader. He also stands alone as a person. In the Bible, there are over 300 prophecies about His first coming to planet Earth. Professor Peter Stoner, in his book, SCIENCE SPEAKS, sheds a floodlight of insight onto the incredibility of those 300 prophecies. He led a team of people in projecting the odds against just eight of those prophecies happening to one person, without God directly causing them.

The eight prophecies Stoner selected were: 1) place of birth, 2) announced by a forerunner, 3) entering Jerusalem on a donkey, 4) betrayal by a friend resulting in hand wounds, 5) betrayed for 30 pieces of silver, 6) the 30 pieces of silver thrown on the temple floor and given to buy a potter's field, 7) made no defense for self, and, 8) was crucified.

Professor Stoner's team used mathematical calculations to determine what the chances were of each prophecy happening to the same person, with each prophecy building on the prophecies before it.

Here's the chance, Stoner concluded, that all eight of those prophecies could be fulfilled in the same person, without God causing them to happen. He found it was the same chance a blindfolded person would have in selecting a marked silver dollar, out of a two-foot deep pile of silver dollars, covering the entire state of Texas, on the *first* try! Make no mistake about it. Jesus was unlike anyone who has ever lived!

When I was a kid, someone quoted John 10:10 to me. In this passage, Jesus said, "I came that you might have life, and have it more abundantly." Well, I was into abundance. I liked that word, as long as it was attached to something good. So, Jesus' bold claim struck the right chord with me.

What I have learned from Him since then, I have passed on to others in the sport and business worlds, as well as to staff of different organizations. Even to parents. I am still a student of Jesus, learning from Him most every day. This book comes from many years of going "on the road" with Jesus, through the pages of the Bible. And, for me, it has been an incredible adventure.

The Follower-Leader

Would you do me one big favor, as we set out on this journey? Would you set aside what you already think about Jesus? That's right, mentally set it aside. No, not that I can persuade you a certain way. But that He can, one way or another. Let the chips of opinion fall where they might, as you walk with Jesus on each page.

If you've come to this book with years and years of experience in leading, great. However, as a leader, you know how important it is to keep learning. As you go "on the road" with Jesus in this book, you'll be learning from the best. In fact, from the greatest.

If you've come to this book, and you are "just" an ordinary person, and you have no aspirations for leadership, take another look. Are you a parent? When your first baby was born, you graduated from the "ordinary" into being a leader. You remember playing "Follow the Leader" as a kid. Well, guess who is following you? Yes, as a parent, you're a leader.

Are you an athlete, or an employee, or, "just" living in a neighborhood? Again, look around. Any place there are people, there are eyes looking at you. Do you model what you believe? Are your actions consistent with your values? The bottom line? You are a leader. The question is, what kind of a leader?

If you've come to this book, and you don't even know if God exists, relax, and enjoy the trip. If God does exist, He'll get through to you, and you'll know it. If you've come to this book, and you're skeptical about Jesus, that's okay. A couple of His men were born skeptics. When you're traveling with Him through this book, if He is who He has claimed to be, He Himself will let you know. Jesus was the ultimate Follower-Leader.

First, He was a devoted follower of His Father. You will later read that Jesus said He didn't say or do anything without being totally in line with His Father. He was a follower all the way to His death on the cross.

Second, because He was a great follower, He was also a great leader. He knew where He was going, and other people tagged along with Him. That's leadership. In fact, people are "tagging along" with Him all around the world. That's great leadership.

You also have been designed by God to be a Follower-Leader. No matter if you see yourself as a leader, or have never thought of yourself as being a leader, it doesn't matter. Being a Follower-Leader is the destiny God has for you.

As you go on the road with Jesus, He will show you how to follow Him, and He will show you how to lead others. That's right. He will teach you, and show you, how to do it. Only then, as you become the Follower-Leader God has designed you to be, will you experience the "abundant life," in John 10:10, Jesus said He came to give.

May I suggest a plan for incorporating the tips Jesus modeled into your life? You can modify the plan to better meet your own needs, and time schedule. But, to get you started, here's the strategy I believe will work the best:

First, set some time aside each day, to read a portion of this book. Do that until you get the entire book read, tips included. No, you don't have to ponder the discussion questions at this first reading.

You don't even have to look up the Bible references. That will come later. This first reading is just to give you an overview, a preview of your journey ahead. A "get-the-feel" run-through.

"Wait a minute," you might say, "how can reading the entire book be nothing but an overview?" Believe me, you'll discover the answer to that question as you carry out the second part of the plan.

Next, in the "On the Road" section, take just one page at a time. That's right. No more than one page a day. Read the page. Then, read the account out of the Bible for more details, and a fuller version.

Finally, ponder the questions. Either alone, or in a group with others. Talk with God about the questions. Ask Him how He wants to implement that particular tip in your life.

Then, rely on Him to help you do it.

Now, let's revisit the question on the back cover.

"What would change in the next six months
if you patterned everything you said and did
after the man considered to be the greatest
leader who ever lived?

Well, after reading about the "meeting place," on the next
four pages, you'll start finding out for yourself. You're in for
one incredible adventure!

The Meeting Place

A few years ago, I was sitting in Jack Herschend's office at Silver Dollar City, a world-renown theme park in Branson, Missouri. Jack, along with his brother, Pete, are co-owners of the park. That afternoon, Jack told me something that I logged in the back of my mind. I was writing an article about him, at the time, so I happened to record exactly what he said. Today, I understand even better the value of his concept.

"Not long after my brother, Pete, turned his life over to the Lord," Jack said, as he casually leaned back in his easy chair, "he came into my office and told me about it. We sat there for awhile just grinning at each other. Then I said, 'Well, I suppose if something is changing our lives, we ought to let it spill over into the way we do business.'

"Pete replied, 'Maybe we should ask the Lord to help us decide how to run things. Shall we have an executive meeting and invite Him to attend?'

"We decided to use the woods behind the Wilderness Church at Silver Dollar City as our 'conference room.' We walked out together and sat on an old log, surrounded by the beauty of the winter landscape. We prayed, 'Lord, show us how our faith should shape our lives, and our business.'

"That was the first of many 'executive meetings' on that log over the years. And that's how we still make our major decisions today."

Several years later, my wife and I left the beautiful Ozark hills of Branson for the greenery of central Ohio. In walking the woods near our condo, I discovered a "meeting place" similar to Jack and Pete's outdoor "conference room," where they sat on their old log.

Most every morning, my wife and I take a walk through those woods. As we leave the condo, for the first several yards, we talk together, appreciating nature. We see an occasional wild turkey, or a deer darting between the trees.

Then, at a certain point, we turn on our iPods and go it "alone." I usually listen to an audio book. But, after about 600 yards of hiking on the trail, coming up on my "meeting place," I turn off the audio book. Sometimes, I turn on some Bill Gaither music; other times I leave the sound off altogether. As I walk between the two "guard" trees, at the entrance of my "meeting place," I feel I'm entering into the presence of God.

Oh, other hikers pass right on through that 40-yard long opening when they're on the trail. But, they might not be paying as much attention to the grandeur of the tall trees, or the many interesting crevices in the fallen dead trees, or even in the many different kinds of shrubs.

To me, those are not just the handiwork of God, although they definitely are that. It's like when I really study all of His creation in that wooded "meeting place," I sense a stronger presence of God. I tend to appreciate Him even more.

In that "meeting place," I have talked with God many times about the content of this book. He has given me insights into many of the different teachings and life experiences of Jesus. Insights that I didn't have before I talked with Him. He also has helped me see where I have been falling short in my own partnering with Jesus, and how I can improve.

But, mostly, in that "meeting place," I feel a oneness with God. He accepts me, and I accept Him. No longer do I want Him to put His blessing, or "stamp of approval" on what I'm doing. I simply want to be caught up in His agenda, in what He's doing. I figure it doesn't get any better than that.

In fact, as a result of one of my morning get-togethers with the Lord, my desire has been that you might find "going on the road" with Jesus through the pages of this book to be a special "meeting place" for you. A time of your day when you can kick back a little, and tune out the cares of the world for a few minutes. A time when you can connect with God so that the rest of your day will be an even greater experience for you. A time when Jesus Himself will be your mentor in helping you become the Follower-Leader God has designed you to be.

That time in my "meeting place' is the best part of my day. It's no longer a discipline for me to spend time with the Lord. Now, I look forward to it each morning, and I greatly miss it when I don't do it.

As I wrote earlier, I think reading the entire book through is the best way to start. But, that is only a start. Then, I think it's best, to come back, and take it just one page at a time. Get into your "meeting place" with the Lord. Read the page, read the portion out of your Bible. Then, ponder the questions for discussion, talking with God about what He wants you to do about it. I'm hoping that Jack and Pete's prayer will be your own special request of the Lord:

> "Lord, show us how our faith should shape
> our lives, and our business."

May each encounter with "the greatest leader who ever lived," on the pages of this book, be for you what the log has been for the Herschend brothers, and my "meeting place" has been for me. May you become the Follower-Leader God has designed you to be.

The world is in need of what you have to offer.

Now, with that said, let's hit the road.

ON THE ROAD
WITH JESUS

YEAR ONE

DEDICATED TO
THE "FABULOUS FIVE"

This section is in honor of five men, who are definitely the "Fabulous Five." Ed Belveal, Andy Compton, Chris Stange, Wes Stoner, and Craig White. Five men who, in different eras, I have met with weekly. Three of whom I had been meeting with for about 15 years, before Peggy and I moved away from Branson. You men have played a big part in my motivation to keep trekking along "on the road" with Jesus. And, you've added so much to my insight into His teachings, and life experiences.

In this section, we start our journey with Jesus. In it, we'll see Him recruit a team, and start casting the vision to each of His men, ending up this year with only seven that we know about, along with a huge number of curious seekers. Each of you men are also great "recruiters" for getting people "on the road" with Jesus. You give them a chance to make their own minds up about Him.

GOD ENTERS THE WORLD

LUKE 1:26-55 AND 2:1-11

It happened in a pile of straw on the dirt floor of a smelly Palestinian barn. No trumpets blowing. No press corps camping out front. Just a few cows and sheep looking on.

A baby was born.

The newborn was nothing special to look at. Nothing that would let the few cows and sheep get the picture of how great that baby would become. Yet, what happened that morning on a small planet in one medium-sized galaxy, out of at least a couple of hundred billion other galaxies throughout the universe...yes, what happened that morning...it was very special.

LEADERSHIP TIP #1

Enter into the world of each person you lead with your mind and emotions, as well as your physical presence.

The invisible God who created the entire, incomprehensible universe out of nothing, the same God who holds it all together for His pleasure...that God entered into life in a visible way, and for His unique purpose. In that one great act, God Himself became the model for empathy. He fully entered into the world of His own creation. A baby was born. A baby who would grow into a man. Yet, a man like no other.

1. Why is it important for a leader to enter into the world of those he leads?

2. How can you train your people to enter into the world of others?

THE BALANCED LIFE

LUKE 2:52

The Bible doesn't contain much information on Jesus growing up. However, we do have one story about Him, when He was twelve years old. He and His parents, along with His brothers and sisters, traveled to Jerusalem for the Passover celebration. Now, it was routine, in those days, because of bandits robbing travelers on the road, for people to travel in a large group of other people for protection.

> **LEADERSHIP TIP #2**
>
> Maintain a proper balance between your mental, physical, spiritual, and social dimensions.

After the Passover celebration, both of Jesus' parents had individually joined up with the traveling group with their other children. Each parent thought their older son, Jesus, was with the other one. Little did they realize He was still back in the temple. He was engaged in a challenging conversation with the brilliant religious teachers. Challenging for the teachers, that is. Not for the twelve year old Jesus. After that episode, we don't know much about what happened. We only know He grew in wisdom, physical size, and He was well liked by both people and God. In other words, Jesus lived a balanced life.

1. Why is balance in life important for a leader?

2. What steps can you take to improve the balance in your life?

His Time Had Come

MATTHEW 3:13-17

When Jesus was in His early thirties, news about John the Baptist had spread like wildfire across the land. John had been crying out for the Jewish people to repent of their sins, both against God and their fellow man. And, as an outward sign of their repentance, John

LEADERSHIP TIP #3

Be alert to God's leading.

had been calling those people who repented to be baptized.

Perhaps it happened while Jesus was fixing an oxcart wheel in His carpenter shop. Maybe that's when His Father impressed Him to travel the 70 miles south to be baptized by John. But, why would Jesus even need to be baptized? He had no sin from which to repent. Yet, He knew that was how His Father wanted Him to start His mission. His time had come.

At sunrise, within a couple of days, His family probably walked with Him to the edge of Nazareth, and stood with Him overlooking the plains below. Then, some warm embraces, and Jesus was on His way, hiking down the dirt road to the main highway below. Destination, a meeting up with John.

1. What does it mean to be alert to God's leading?

2. Based on what you already know, what are some ways you can be more alert to God's leading in your life?

THE RIVER EXPERIENCE

MATTHEW 3:13-17, MARK 1:9-11, AND LUKE 3:21-22

After three days on the road, Jesus knew He was getting close to John. He could see people hiking up a rocky trail, through a dense growth of shrubs and trees. Jesus took off down that same trail, and soon came to a clearing by the river. People were standing on the banks in

> **LEADERSHIP TIP #4**
>
> Openly identify with God and His right way of doing things.

drenched clothes, warmly embracing each other. Others were circled around the full-bearded man in the water, the man dressed in a camel's hair garment.

As John finished baptizing his last person, Jesus stepped into the river. John looked over at Jesus, wading toward him. Then, suddenly, it hit him. John raised his arms in front, gesturing for Jesus to stop. "Why are you coming to me?" he asked. "I am the one who should be baptized by you."

Jesus kept pushing through the water toward John, and said, "No. You baptize me. It's the right thing to do." John agreed, and lowered and raised Jesus in the water. In that act, Jesus knew He had done what His Father wanted Him to do. It was His way of openly identifying with Him. It was right.

> What ways can you openly identify with God in your work, and in your community?

Battle in the Wilderness

Matthew 4:1-11 and Luke 4:1-13

As Jesus waded out of the Jordan River, the Spirit of God compelled Him to hike into the Judean Wilderness. That was a desolate stretch of land to the east of the Dead Sea. It was there that Satan would try his best to keep Jesus from the mission God had given Him.

LEADERSHIP TIP #5

Take time to mentally and spiritually prepare for each task of the day, making sure you are tuned into God.

During the entire forty days, Jesus went without food. In the eerie quietness of that land, He could hear the howling of roving hyenas at night. At day, the parched ground crackling under His sandals. Jesus could also hear, in His mind, two distinct voices. One coming from Satan in his ongoing attempts to sidetrack Him. The other coming from His Father, who kept encouraging Him.

It was a time of intense mental and spiritual preparation for a mission only He could carry out. Then, in the last days, after failing to get Jesus off course, Satan came at Him with three great temptations. Each was designed as a knockout punch.

1. Why is it important to take a moment to prepare before engaging in even a routine task?

2. Before a task, how can you tune into God?

Stones Into Bread

MATTHEW 4:1-11 AND LUKE 4:1-13

Satan waited until the forty days without food had weakened Jesus physically. Then, with Jesus at His weakest point, Satan thought he could get Him off course. How? By tempting Jesus to use His power to satisfy His growing hunger.

LEADERSHIP TIP #6

Use your resources and abilities for the good of others rather than simply for yourself.

"If you are the Son of God," Satan said, "turn these stones into bread." Now, that was not really an "iffy" challenge. You see, the word, "if," in the first-class condition, as Satan used it, means, "If... and it is true." Satan knew who Jesus was. He was tempting Jesus to use His power, as the Son of God, to satisfy His own hunger. That, of course, would take a miracle.

However, Jesus knew the purpose of the miracles. They were to prove who He was to other people, and to help others, not to satisfy His own desires. In the wilderness, because no one else was present, there was no reason for a miracle. So Jesus kept relying on His Father to give Him the strength to see Him through. And, He used Scripture to say "No" to Satan.

How can you better use your resources for others as well as yourself and your family?

No Compromise

MATTHEW 4:1-11 AND LUKE 4:1-13

Satan failed in his first "knockout" temptation. But, he wasn't through. He told Jesus to climb a high mountain in the wilderness. So, Jesus, weakened by no food, slowly and painfully climbed to the top. Then, standing, with a gentle breeze cooling His sweaty forehead, Jesus looked out over the land. He could see all the way to the blue, Mediterranean Sea.

LEADERSHIP TIP #7

Hold fast to God's values in your place of work, regardless of the pressures put on you to compromise.

All of a sudden, Satan put into Jesus' mind a dazzling display of wealth and world power. Interestingly, Satan claimed all of what Jesus "saw," were his to give. Jesus never questioned that claim. He knew it was true.

Now, Satan was clever in this temptation. He hit Jesus at the heart of His mission. Satan would help Jesus win the world without Jesus ever going to the cross. All He would have to do was bend a knee to the ground in honor of Satan. No one else would have to know. What was wrong with that? Just this. He would be compromising loyalty to His Father. Once again, He used Scripture to defeat the tempting offer.

What steps can you take to avoid compromising God's values in specific situations?

25

SATAN'S PLOY ON A LEDGE

MATTHEW 4:1-11 AND LUKE 4:1-13

Satan was no dummy. He noticed that Jesus' strength was in His reliance on Scripture. So, with a trick in mind, Satan led Jesus down the mountain, across the barren land, and into Jerusalem. He took Him to the very gate of the temple itself.

It was early in the morning, and a priest had just

> ### LEADERSHIP TIP #8
>
> Line up your plans with God's words in the Bible, keeping them in context, to avoid making bad decisions, expecting God to bail you out.

stood in a tower of the temple, blowing his trumpet. The blast signaled a new day for worshipping God had begun. Along with hundreds of other people, Jesus walked through the courtyard. He was heading toward the stairs leading up to the tower. He slowly climbed those stairs. Once at the top, Satan encouraged Jesus to inch closer to the edge. He did. And, from the edge, Jesus saw all the people milling below.

"Jump off," Satan prodded, "for it is written…" Then he quoted a passage of Scripture, out of context. It was to get Jesus to depend on angels to save Him from certain death. However, Jesus knew Satan was twisting His Father's words to mean something different. "You shall not tempt, the Lord, your God," Jesus boldly shot back. And, Satan struck out.

> What do you think would happen if you, for one year, read a chapter out of Proverbs each day that corresponded to the date of the month?

THE JEWISH DELEGATION

JOHN 1:19-28

While Jesus had been battling Satan in the wilderness, John the Baptist had a visit from a Jewish delegation sent from the temple. It was customary for Jewish religious leaders to check out anybody claiming to be a spokesperson from God. So, after hearing about John,

LEADERSHIP TIP #9

Know who you are not; then, know who you are.

the leaders sent out a delegation to ask him about his qualifications.

Now, John could have boasted about being God's only spokesperson in over 400 years. That's what he was. But, he didn't. He simply answered, "I am a voice, crying in the wilderness, 'Make straight the way of the Lord.'" With that answer, John had picked up on a practice of villages. When a village was expecting a visit from the king, it would send out road crews to fill in potholes. The crews would also straighten the roads to make it an easier ride for the expected king. John saw himself as merely calling people to get ready for true royalty. John knew he wasn't the Messiah. Yet, he knew who he was.

1. Why is it just as important to know who you are not as it is to know who you are?

2. Who aren't you, and who are you?

27

A DAY WITH JESUS

JOHN 1:35-39

Jesus had just returned from His battle in the wilderness, and He was walking along a road near the Jordan River. Off that road, John the Baptist stood with a couple of his own disciples. Men who had taken a leave of absence from their work as fishermen. They, along with their brothers, were

LEADERSHIP TIP #10

Increase your enthusiasm for Jesus by spending time alone with Him each day.

in search of the Messiah who would restore Israel to its greatness. At first, they might have thought John was the Messiah.

However, that morning, as John saw Jesus walking in the distance, he raised his hand, and pointed. "There goes the Lamb of God," he told his men. The two men, Andrew and another John, were intrigued by what John just said. They started out after Jesus, then quickened their pace to catch up to Him. John knew he had just passed the baton from the old to the new.

Andrew and John spent the rest of the day with Jesus in the guest room where He was staying. Then, after getting to know Him better, they both ran off to bring their brothers back to meet Jesus. Their search for the Messiah had ended.

What time of day will you commit to spend alone with Jesus, and what will you do during that time?

A NEW NAME FOR SIMON

JOHN 1:40-42

Andrew brought his brother, Simon, back to the guest room to introduce him to Jesus. As the two brothers walked through the open doorway, Jesus welcomed them.

LEADERSHIP TIP #11

Give only nicknames that will draw out a person's potential.

In fact, Jesus probably untied their sandals and washed their feet. That would have been keeping in line with Jewish hospitality. Then, after drying their feet with a towel, Jesus stood up and looked intently into the very heart of Simon. He could see exactly who Simon was. However, Jesus could also see who Simon could become. That's the person He latched onto.

"You are Simon, son of John," Jesus said, "but you will be called Cephas." (Cephas was Aramaic for Peter, the same name in Greek.) Perhaps it was with a smile, and an affirming nod of His head, that Jesus gave Simon the name of Cephas, or Peter. Quite a new name. It meant "little rock." In spite of the wishy-washy person Simon presently was, Jesus saw in him the solid person he could become.

1. Experiments have shown that people tend to either live up, or live down, to what other people think of them. Why do you think this is true?

2. What nicknames would you give different people you're leading to help them fulfill God's destiny for them?

29

FOLLOW ME

JOHN 1:43-44

Before Jesus had left home, He apparently made a promise to return for a wedding. So He headed north with His four new friends to keep that promise. No doubt, along the four-day journey, Peter and Andrew talked to Jesus about their hometown friend, Philip. The two brothers figured he would be a man who would, also, want to become one of Jesus' followers.

> **LEADERSHIP TIP #12**
>
> Commit yourself to be a follower of Jesus, and a leader in building God's Kingdom through your normal way of life.

Jesus and His men probably walked into town about mid-morning, heading straight to Philip's house. For the next several minutes, they all might have sat inside Philip's house on the packed, dirt floor, eating date loaves, and visiting with their host. Jesus explained He had come to recruit people into God's Kingdom. Philip asked penetrating questions. Jesus gave insightful answers. When Jesus saw that Philip was getting it, He looked him straight in the eyes, and said, "Follow me." It wasn't as if Jesus was going somewhere at that moment. What did He mean, "Follow me."? Philip knew. That day, he made a commitment to go along with Jesus.

1. What does it mean to follow Jesus?

2. What does it mean to be a leader in building God's Kingdom?

Philip Recruits Nathanael

John 1:43-51

Philip asked Jesus to wait while he went to tell his friend, Nathanael about Him. Nathanael was resting under a fig tree when Philip, excitedly, raced toward him. "We've found the one Moses and the prophets wrote about," he called out, probably a little out

> **LEADERSHIP TIP #13**
>
> Invite a skeptic to check Jesus out for himself.

of breath. "His name is Jesus. He comes from Nazareth."

"Nazareth?" Nathanael shot back. Can anything good come out of Nazareth?" he asked, probably with a "know-it-all" smirk. Actually, he had a point. Nazareth had a poor reputation. It wasn't even mentioned in the Old Testament, the only Scriptures the people had. It was an outpost for the Roman army, with all the immorality commonly thought of around an army camp. No way, in Nathanael's mind, the Messiah could possibly come out of Nazareth.

Philip might have wanted to argue with his friend. Perhaps they had argued many times about the issues of life. But, not this time. Instead, Philip wisely said, "Come, and see for yourself." Nathanael did. He became Jesus' sixth follower.

> What's the value of asking a skeptic to check Jesus out for himself instead of arguing with him? How would you go about asking a skeptic to do that?

31

WINE CRISIS AT A WEDDING

JOHN 2:1-12

Shortly after Jesus recruited Philip and Nathanael to follow Him, He and all six of His friends attended a wedding celebration. It was in the small Galilean village of Cana, about three miles from Jesus' hometown.

> **LEADERSHIP TIP #14**
>
> Tell God your concerns, and leave them in His hands to do whatever He thinks is best.

Jewish wedding celebrations lasted up to a week, and they were big social events. People could relax from the Roman tyranny, eat lots of food, enjoy good wine, tell their tall stories and laugh at their favorite jokes. During the week, the newlyweds were responsible for the food and wine. Now, wine was important. It was a sign of hospitality. Having it meant everyone was welcome.

So, in the middle of the week when the wine ran out, it was a huge social blunder. A real crisis. Jesus' mother, Mary, knew she could go to her son with any problem. She quietly told Him about it. However, from Jesus' answer, He implied He wasn't going to do anything. Interestingly, Mary didn't argue. She just left the crisis in His hands to handle it.

Jesus later taught His followers to keep asking for prayer requests (Matthew 7:7-8) . Yet, Mary only presented her need once. How is Jesus' teaching and His mother's method compatible?

FILLING JARS WITH WATER

JOHN 2:1-11

When Mary told Jesus about the wine crisis, He answered, "My time has not yet come." Jesus knew it would take a miracle to produce more wine. It seems He wanted to do His first public miracles, to officially start His work, at the Passover in Jerusalem. That was still a week away.

> **LEADERSHIP TIP #15**
>
> When you see someone who needs help, ask God if He might want you to be flexible with your plans to help that person.

However, Jesus was flexible. He, evidently, changed His mind. As He walked out to the serving galley, He looked around, and saw six large, empty, stone water pots. Each had held water for the Jewish ritual of washing hands before, and in between, the eating of food.

Mary knew her son well. She had already directed the servants to do whatever He told them to do. So, when Jesus instructed them to fill all six water pots to their brims with water, they quickly went into action. They had no clue how the water was going to solve the wine problem. Yet, they kept going to the outside well until all six pots were full. Little did they know what was about to happen to that water.

> If you do change your plans, how can you still be faithful to your prior commitment?

WATER INTO WINE

JOHN 2:1-11

In a split second, Jesus turned 72 gallons of water into 72 gallons of wine. Now, make no mistake, turning water into wine was definitely a miracle. Jesus bypassed the growing, the harvesting, and the processing of the grapes from start to finish. So, why did He perform this miracle when He had refused to

LEADERSHIP TIP #16

When you bring a request to God, keep your eyes open for how He is responding. He might be using what you already have.

turn stones into bread? Well, at the wedding, it was to save His friends from starting their marriage out being humiliated.

Yet, there was even more to this miracle than saving face for His friends. Jesus used something tangible, water, to produce something else tangible, wine. He demonstrated to His followers how God, often, will use resources they already have in answering their prayer requests.

Sometimes, God will just rearrange the resources. Sometimes, He will impress His people how they can use what they have more efficiently. And, sometimes, like with the water, God will add His special touch. It might not always be a miracle. But, it will always be His special touch.

What resources do you presently have that God might use in answering one of your prayer requests?

THE AMAZED GOVERNOR

JOHN 2:1-12

At Jewish weddings, it was customary for one person to be appointed the governor. He was the overseer of the week-long celebration. His job was to make sure the party was running smoothly. Included in his responsibilities was the tasting of wine before it was served to the guests. In this pleasurable duty, he had to make sure the wine was up to a certain standard.

> **LEADERSHIP TIP #17**
>
> Challenge the people you're leading to always give better than what's expected of them, regardless of the situation.

Now, the richer quality of wine was normally served at the start of the week. Then, after people had been eating and drinking for a few days, their taste buds would have grown a bit dull. That's when the poorer quality of wine was served.

However, in tasting the wine the servants had just brought to him -- the wine Jesus had produced -- the governor was surprised. It was actually a better quality than the first batch of wine. Jesus had given better than He had to. And, far better than anyone had expected. So, the governor sent for the bridegroom to do some explaining. A lot the bridegroom knew.

> As a model for your people, how can you give better than you presently are giving?

THE RIP-OFF ARTISTS

JOHN 2:12-22

Right after the wedding in Cana, Jesus and His men spent time relaxing with Peter and his family. Then, it was off to the Passover celebration in Jerusalem. At this festival, all Jewish males, 19 years of age and older, were obliged to pay a tax with Jewish coins. The tax was used to maintain

LEADERSHIP TIP #18

Using self-control, allow yourself to be angry only when people are defaming God.

the temple and its many services. Several weeks before the event, money-changers would set up stalls in the outlying villages. That was to enable people to exchange their Gentile money for the mandatory Jewish coins.

Many people didn't make that switch-over before the Passover. So, the money-changers set up shop in the outer temple court to offer their services during the festival. However, not for the normal profit. Now, they charged a huge profit margin. They also gave a kick-back of their profit to the temple priests for allowing them to be there. It was that high rate that stirred up loud arguments. Those arguments caused a big distraction for anyone trying to worship God. Jesus saw what was going on, and anger burned within Him. He kicked them all out.

How will you determine what is defaming God, and what isn't, in your quest to control your anger?

KNOWING PEOPLE'S HEARTS

JOHN 2:23-25

Jesus didn't just kick the rip-off merchants out of the temple courtyard. He also performed many miracles at the start of the celebration. Because of those miracles, people were naturally attracted to Him.

LEADERSHIP TIP #19

Don't rely on a person to be loyal to you if he has associated with you for hidden motives.

We don't know exactly what He did, but, when people saw Him do them, they were impressed. Perhaps He cured some incurable diseases. We just don't know.

Jesus used His miracles to confirm who He was. To get people to accept His message of God's love and forgiveness. Now, it was good the people were impressed. But, Jesus wasn't calling them just to be awed by His power. He was calling them to experience a new and exciting, one-on-one, relationship with the Creator of the universe. However, Jesus knew what was in the people's hearts. He knew they wanted more miracles. He also knew they would be fickle in their allegiance to Him. They weren't following for the right reason. They simply saw Him as a "good show." He was definitely that.

1. How can you determine what a person's motives are?

2. What will you look for in the people you're leading?

A LATE NIGHT CONVERSATION

JOHN 3:1-21

It happened late one night during the Passover. The great Jewish teacher, Nicodemus, was slipping in and out of the shadows cast by the full moon, as he walked down a quiet street. He was heading toward the room where Jesus was staying. Apparently, Nicodemus had earlier blended in with the huge masses of people who had been crowding around Jesus. Like the others, he listened to every word, and watched every miracle. And, like the others, he was impressed.

> **LEADERSHIP TIP #20**
>
> Develop a notebook of physical realities that illustrate the values you want to teach the people you're leading.

Nicodemus must have been afraid of being "blackballed" by his fellow teachers of religious law if he talked with Jesus. He couldn't risk talking with Him in broad daylight. So, Nicodemus climbed the outside stairs to Jesus' packed-out guest room, a room Jesus was sharing with His family and friends. Jesus gladly welcomed the great teacher at the late hour. However, He immediately challenged his guest's way of thinking. Jesus used physical realities, like child-birth and the wind whistling through the streets, to illustrate spiritual realities.

> What values do you want to get across to the people you lead, and what physical realities can you use to illustrate those values?

NEW BIRTH NEEDED

JOHN 3:3

When Jesus told Nicodemus he had to be "born again" to experience the Kingdom of God, that was beyond his grasp. Jewish people understood the need for Gentiles to be "born again." That's how they converted to Judaism. But, no Jewish person ever thought he had to have a new birth.

> **LEADERSHIP TIP #21**
>
> Make the issue of your people spending eternity with God your top priority.

Certainly, no great Jewish teacher, like Nicodemus.

Now, Nicodemus was either confused, or embarrassed, that Jesus thought he had to be born again. It just didn't make sense to him. So, he asked a silly question, like, "How can a grown man get back into his mother's womb, only to come out again?" Jesus might have smiled at the question. But, He pressed on with His explanation.

One birth was physical, the second, or new, birth was spiritual. Both were just as real. And, both were needed for a person to enjoy God's Forever Kingdom. Not even the great Jewish teacher, Nicodemus, was exempt from that reality.

> How would you feel if one of your family members, or people you lead, didn't get to spend eternity with God because you didn't tell them about Jesus?

Love is Action

John 3:16

In the conversation Jesus had with Nicodemus, Bible scholars are divided as to who actually uttered the famous words, "For God so loved the world, He gave His only begotten Son, that whoever believes in Him shall not perish, but have eternal life." Some say it was Jesus. Others say it was John, the author of the book in which it was written.

> **LEADERSHIP TIP #22**
>
> In specific actions, express God's love to your family members and to the people you lead.

Actually, it really doesn't matter which of the two men said it. The point is, it's part of God's Word, so basically, it's God saying it.

John 3:16 is the message God wants all followers of Jesus to articulate and model. Because of God's love for the world, He took action. He brought the world into a family relationship with Him, for all eternity. That action is through Jesus. All He said, and all He did. Especially what He did on the cross. So, it boils down to just three words:

Love is action.

> What actions can you take to show God's love to your family and the people you lead?

JEALOUSY IN THE AIR

JOHN 3:22-30

After the Passover, Jesus spent some time with His men near the river where John used to baptize. Meanwhile, John had moved to another area. People had been intrigued with Jesus in Jerusalem. Now, they were coming to learn more. Many of them responded to His message, and they wanted to be baptized. So, Jesus allowed His men to baptize the people. He Himself didn't baptize anyone.

LEADERSHIP TIP #23

Avoid being jealous of others by being committed to what God has called you to do.

Someone wanted to stir up a little trouble. So, he told the disciples of John the Baptist that Jesus was baptizing more than John. Fired up by jealousy, the men ran to their leader and complained about what Jesus was doing.

However, John wasn't jealous at all. In fact, he was thrilled people were streaming to Jesus. Just like they used to rush out to him. John knew, if that was happening, then he was doing his job. Pointing people to Jesus. John was happy. Not one jealous bone in his body.

1. What's the difference between being respectful of other leaders, and being jealous of them?

2. How can focusing on what God has called you to do keep you from being jealous of others?

41

INCREASING AND DECREASING

JOHN 3:22-30

John's disciples most likely couldn't figure out their leader's calmness in hearing about all the people Jesus was reported to be baptizing. To them, it was like an upstart carpenter from Nazareth taking over the "family business."

LEADERSHIP TIP #24

Set aside time each day to increase Jesus in your life.

Hey, where were they when their leader spoke about Jesus? Didn't they wonder where Andrew and John had gone? How could they have missed what The Baptist was all about? Andrew and John sure didn't. Others didn't. That's why more and more people were heading out to Jesus. It was because John was pointing them in His direction.

How could these few disciples have so badly missed the purpose God had given their leader? Go figure. Yet, what a great opportunity it was for John to hit home. He told them how he saw his partnership with that "upstart" carpenter.

He put it this way. "He must increase, and I must decrease." That's true humility. John knew his role. He pursued it relentlessly.

What are three ways you can "increase" Jesus in your life?

WOMAN AT THE WELL

JOHN 4:1-42

While Jesus and His men were in the Jerusalem area, He heard that John had been arrested. So, for Jesus' safety, His Father directed Him to get out of the area, and head north to Galilee.

> ## LEADERSHIP TIP #25
>
> Relying on the strength of Jesus in you, give of yourself to help others, even when you're tired.

Jesus and His men had been walking for several hours in the hot sun when they came to Jacob's Well in Samaria. It was a place where many travelers would stop to get refreshed. Interestingly, this is the only place in the Bible where we read Jesus was both hungry and tired.

God, apparently, told Jesus to stay behind while His men hiked into the village to buy supplies. It was about a half mile away. So, Jesus rested at the well, perhaps sitting on the ground, leaning against a tree while His men were gone. Soon, an outcast woman came all the way to the well to draw water. For a few minutes, Jesus studied her gloomy expression. Then, in spite of being tired, He got to His feet and started a conversation with her. He wanted to help her connect to God.

> 1. What experience have you had in God impressing you to do something, like Jesus staying at the well?
>
> 2. How can Jesus help you give of yourself, even when you're tired?

43

A POINT OF CONTACT

JOHN 4:1-42

Jewish people and Samaritans had nothing to do with each other. They were bitter enemies. Therefore, it would have been more natural for the Jewish Jesus *not* to have said anything to the Samaritan woman.

> **LEADERSHIP TIP #26**
>
> Use a mutual-interest point of contact to start a conversation that can help your people look at a truth or value you want to communicate.

To make matters worse, men did not speak to women in public. That just was not allowed. Yet, Jesus had not been walking the land conforming to how it had always been done. He was ushering in a new way, His Father's way, to show how it should be done.

Now, since Jesus had chosen to help the woman, how would He open up a conversation with her? He decided to use an interest He and she both shared. Water. He simply said, "Give me a drink." Then, after a brief exchange, Jesus used the water, again, to talk to the woman about "living water." He was referring to Himself. Water was His point of contact. He started talking with the woman about truths of eternal consequences, using a mutual-interest point of contact.

> What are some mutual-interest points of contact you can use to communicate your values to those you are leading?

44

AN ENERGY BOOST

JOHN 4:1-42

Just as Jesus seemed to be getting through to the stubborn and hard-headed woman, His disciples walked up with the supplies. Talk about bad timing. Yet, as the episode plays out, we see that His time with the woman really did take root in her heart. She brought many of the villagers out to meet Jesus, and they invited Him to stay over in their village. After four days with Jesus, many of the villagers believed in Him. They saw Him as their promised Messiah. Meanwhile, back at the well.

> ## LEADERSHIP TIP #27
>
> Keep refreshing your mind with God's words, and you'll experience His energy.

As the woman ran off, one of Jesus' men offered Him something to eat. That was only natural since Jesus was hungry and tired when they left Him. But Jesus turned down the offer. Now, that didn't make sense. Why didn't Jesus need food when His followers returned? He explained it this way, "I have food you don't know about." Okay, what food was He talking about? The food of His Father's words He spoke to the woman. He was energized in speaking those words, and in doing what His Father wanted Him to do (Matthew 4:4).

> How does being caught up in being a conduit for God's words give you energy to do what He wants you to do?

An "Unreasonable" Command

John 4:43-54

After their four day stay in the Samaritan village, Jesus and His men walked to Cana in Galilee. Meanwhile, in Capernaum, some 25 miles away, the son of a grief-stricken government official was about to die. All the medical help didn't work, and the poor father didn't know what to do. Apparently, he had just

> **LEADERSHIP TIP #28**
>
> When you read the Bible, even though you don't completely understand what you're reading, take God at His word, and you'll experience His results.

heard Jesus was back in Cana, the place of His first miracle. So, in desperation, the man took off in his chariot to bring Jesus back with him to heal his son.

As the dust was settling from reining in his horses, and with the man kneeling on the dirt road pleading for Jesus to return with him, Jesus told the man to go back home without him. His son would live. Now, that didn't make sense. Bringing the "Miracle-Worker" back with him was his last hope to keep his son alive. Yet, the man calmly got to his feet, and climbed back into his chariot without Jesus. True to Jesus' word, the boy returned to health at the exact time Jesus said he would.

> What would happen if, according to John 15:7, you took Jesus at His word with a specific request lined up with what He would ask in your situation?

Rejection in Nazareth

LUKE 4:14-30

After His visit to Cana, Jesus traveled throughout Galilee, and then headed home to Nazareth. Word had already reached His friends and neighbors of what He had done for the Gentile, government of-ficial from Capernaum. So, they were looking forward to a few miracles coming their way, too. As a guest teacher in the

LEADERSHIP TIP #29

Every now and then, as you confer with Jesus, change your strategy, when needed, to assure greater success in what God has called you to do.

synagogue, Jesus had just read about the Messiah. Then, look-ing up at His townspeople, He said, "This Scripture has come true today before your very eyes!" Some nodded approval, but probably didn't get what He meant.

However, when Jesus said He wouldn't do any miracles in Nazareth. the people were furious. They rushed forward and mobbed Him, dragging Him out to the edge of a cliff. They intended to shove Him off, but God freed Him. Jesus, then, strategically, decided to move on to Capernaum where people would receive Him better.

1. What situation are you presently facing in which you might need to change your strategy?

2. How can you train the people you're leading to develop back-up plans?

47

CASTING A VISION

MARK 1:16-20

The morning after Jesus had walked into Capernaum, He waited on a plateau, overlooking the lake. He was waiting for His four friends to return from their night of fish-ing. When He saw them, He hiked down a slope to where Peter and Andrew were wading in the lake beside their boat. They were trying to throw

> **LEADERSHIP TIP #30**
>
> Give your people a mental picuture of using their abilities and experi-ences beyond what they're presently doing, to change lives forever.

a small, circular net over a few fish they had spotted. Jesus might have smiled at their unsuccessful attempts. But, He also liked what He saw. They kept after it. Then Jesus called out, "Follow me, and I'll help you catch men."

His voice surprised the two brothers. They looked up and hur-riedly splashed out of the water to embrace their friend. After-ward, the three men walked a bit further down the shoreline to find James and John. Jesus called out the same challenge to them. In a matter of minutes, Jesus had given His friends a vi-sion. A vision to use their skills as fishermen to do something of never-ending value. Something beyond what they were presently doing. A vision to change lives.

> How will you challenge specific people to pursue a mission, beyond what they're presently doing, to change lives for all eternity?

TROUBLE IN THE SYNAGOGUE

LUKE 4:33-37

Philip and Nathanael were probably staying home while their four friends traveled with Jesus around Galilee. Every place Jesus and His men went, they brought God's message of hope to the people. One Sabbath, they were in the Capernaum synagogue where Jesus was teaching. As usual, it was going well. Then,

LEADERSHIP TIP #31

A close partnership with Jesus will help you be calm and unafraid when you're challenged by someone, or something.

suddenly, seemingly out of nowhere, a man crazed with a demon shocked the audience. He shouted out, "Ha, what do you want with us, Jesus of Nazareth? I know who you are. Have you come here to destroy us?"

The people sitting near the man probably scrambled out of his way. But Jesus wasn't caught off guard. Instead of flinching, He stood His ground, and took control. "Come out of him," Jesus commanded. At those words, the demon threw the man to the ground, convulsed him, and left him lying like a rung-out rag. People ran out of the synagogue, spreading the word about a new teacher in town with eye-opening authority.

1. How can staying connected to Jesus keep you calm?

2. How will you stay connected to Jesus throughout the day?

49

PETER'S MOTHER-IN-LAW

LUKE 4:38-39

After the uproar in the synagogue, Peter invited Jesus and His friends to spend, what was left of the Sabbath, resting up at his house. Most likely, on their walk home, Peter told Jesus about his sick mother-in-law.

> **LEADERSHIP TIP #32**
>
> See yourself as a conduit for God's compassion to flow to others.

She evidently had a fever similar to malaria. Not only was she still sick, the fever had drained all of her energy. She was like a wet noodle. Even after her type of fever was broken, it would take quite a few days just to start feeling better. After that, it would take even more days to regain her strength. So, she was one very wiped-out lady.

When Jesus walked into the house, He went directly to the sick woman's bedside. Perhaps, with a weak smile, she nodded a greeting. Then, as Jesus gently took her hand, healing power surged from Him into her. Amazingly, she jumped to her feet, totally well, and fully energized. In fact, she felt so good, she walked into the kitchen and started to fix a meal for all the hungry men. She had to be feeling good for that.

1. What are three examples of conduits?

2. What can you do to show God's compassion for the people you lead?

50

HEALINGS AFTER SUNDOWN

LUKE 4:40-41

Jesus and His companions were relaxing at Peter's house, enjoying a good meal. At the same time, because of how He had healed the demoniac, He had become the talk of the town.

LEADERSHIP TIP #33

Help people sense their importance by giving them individual attention, even in group situations.

As sick people heard the news, it gave them hope. Many of them wanted to be healed. However, no one could go to Jesus yet. You see, being healed on the Sabbath was against the Sabbath law. So, people had to wait until two stars appeared in the sky. Those two stars would officially end the Sabbath. No doubt, every sick person in town was keeping an eagle-eye out for those two stars.

Within minutes after the stars appeared, sick people were jamming into the courtyard of Peter's house. Probably even overflowing into the street. Jesus heard the commotion, and He walked to the open door. When He saw all the people, He had compassion for them. He walked out into the crowd, and took time to heal each person with a word and a touch.

1. Why didn't Jesus just heal everybody at once?

2. How is it possible to give individual attention to people in a group situation?

51

Praying Before Dawn

LUKE 4:42

Jesus didn't have to heal the people in Peter's courtyard one at a time. Yet, He did. And, with each healing, a small amount of energy drained from His body. Finally, after, perhaps, three or four hours, Jesus was exhausted.

> **LEADERSHIP TIP #34**
>
> Begin each new day in close fellowship with God.

In fact, no one was more tired than Jesus when, later that night, He and His men unrolled their guest sleeping mats, stretched them out on the hard-packed dirt floor, and quickly dozed off. Now, you would think Jesus would have slept in the next morning. No one would have blamed Him. But, He didn't.

Instead, before sunrise, Jesus silently climbed to His feet, tiptoed over and around His snoozing friends, left the house and walked to an isolated area where He talked with his Father in prayer. Most likely, that was His daily practice. It was His time to get recharged for the day. A time to take His concerns to His Father. A time to get His next assignment.

> 1. Jesus prayed throughout the day. So, why was setting time aside to be with His Father the first thing He did important to Him?
>
> 2. What can you do to make starting your day in prayer a top priority?

52

THE BEST OVER THE GOOD

MARK 1:35-38

The sun began to rise as Jesus was still in prayer. And, as the sun rose, so did the eager townspeople. Within a short time, more sick people were limping along, and being carried over, to Peter's house. All of them were looking for a touch from Jesus. Peter and his friends must have been

> **LEADERSHIP TIP #35**
>
> Choose the highest priority God has for you, at a specific moment, over other good things you could also do.

excited about the possibility of Jesus setting up "shop" at the house. Then, people could come to Him, maybe from all over the region. Jesus wouldn't even have to go on the road again. So, an enthused Peter went searching for Jesus to let Him know of the good news.

Yet, when Peter found Jesus, no doubt he was surprised by His decision. Jesus told His friend He wanted to go on to other villages. He was sent to bring people the "best news" of His Father's love and forgiveness, not simply to heal them. That was a tough call. Healing people would have been good. However, after spending time in prayer with His Father, Jesus chose the best over the good. Jesus knew His purpose. He stuck to it.

1. What are some good things in your work, and what are the best?

2. How can you know what God's priority is for you?

TEACHING FROM A BOAT

LUKE 5:1-3

Jesus and His men toured Galilee, yet they continued to use Peter's house as their home base. That was convenient, since Peter was the only married disciple. At least, that we know about. It helped having a woman's presence in sharing ideas. She and her mother probably also fixed meals for Jesus and His men.

> **LEADERSHIP TIP #36**
>
> Before each task, take a moment to ask God how you can be more effective.

One morning, as Jesus was walking along the lakeshore, people started gathering around Him to hear more from Him. Soon, He and His large following had reached where Peter was cleaning his fishing nets. As the people sat down on the slope to hear Jesus teach, He took the time to be more effective. He decided to create a setting in which He could be better heard by all the people.

Jesus climbed into Peter's boat. Then, He asked His friend to push the boat a short distance off shore. His idea was to use the water, between the boat and the people, to amplify His voice, as it bounced off the water.

A very effective move.

How might you to be more effective in three of your responsibilities?

Setting Sail for the Deep

Luke 5:4-11

Jesus had just finished teaching the people from Peter's boat. Then, He surprised Peter. He turned to His friend and told him to climb in, so Peter did. "Now," Jesus said, "go out where it is deeper and let down your nets, and you will catch many fish."

LEADERSHIP TIP #37

Be alert to God if He wants you to set sail for an assignment in "deeper waters."

Well, to a seasoned fisherman, like Peter, that didn't make sense. The time for fishing was at night when the fish were feeding off bugs at the surface. Then, the fishermen could use their nets to drag the fish into their boats. In broad daylight, the sun would make it too hot for the fish to swim near the surface. No fisherman would set sail to catch fish during the day. Besides, Peter and His friends had been fishing all night, and they didn't have much luck.

In spite of that, Peter answered, "Because it is you telling me, I will do it." Peter sailed out to where Jesus told him to go, even though it didn't make any fishing sense. Not only did Peter catch fish, he had to motion to his partners, James and John, to bring their boat alongside. They helped Peter haul in the best catch of fish he ever had.

In what "deeper waters" might God be wanting you to set sail?

GOD'S PERSONAL TOUCH

LUKE 5:12-16

One day, after the great catch of fish, Jesus and His men were walking through a town. Seemingly out of nowhere, a leper ran up to Jesus, and fell on the road at His feet.

LEADERSHIP TIP #38

Help those you lead feel good about themselves with your sincerely positive words and actions.

Now, leprosy was considered a "dirty" and contagious disease. In fact, no Jewish person was supposed to get within six feet of anyone with leprosy. So, to help people keep that safer distance, a leper was required to yell, "Unclean... unclean!" as a warning. We can only imagine what a poor self-concept lepers had as they shouted it out. The kneeling man, with his open sores, crusted-over eyes, shriveled hands, and a stench only a garbage dump could love, pleaded with Jesus. "If you are willing," he said, "you can make me clean."

Jesus didn't back up to the safe six-foot distance. Instead, He reached down and touched the man on his sore-infested face. Jesus knew the man needed more that just a healing. He needed a personal touch of God's love. A touch of acceptance.

What personal "touches" can you give the people you lead to help them feel better about their contribution to your cause, and to motivate them to make even greater contributions?

A Forced Withdrawal

Luke 5:14-16

Jesus forcefully told the man He had cleansed of leprosy not to tell anyone what He had done for Him. That was a peculiar command from Jesus, wasn't it? And, to say it so emphatically. After all, wasn't the idea to get His message spread? So, why put a muzzle on a man who was genuinely enthused about what Jesus had just done for him?

> **LEADERSHIP TIP #39**
>
> Keep your eyes on the mission God has given you, instead of a "good" thing that can actually sidetrack you.

Well, it makes sense if we're looking through Jesus' eyes. He knew, if the word got out, He would be swamped by sick people. Yes, it would have been good to heal every sick person in the land. Yet, it would also have slowed Jesus down from getting His life-changing message to more people. Jesus was only interested in getting His message out. Eternity was at stake for people. Unfortunately, the former leper couldn't stop talking about what Jesus had done for him. Because so many people came, searching Him out, Jesus often had to withdraw to the wilderness for prayer, and to let it blow over.

1. How can you maintain a sharp focus on what God has called you to do?

2. How can you help those you're leading maintain a sharp focus on their mission?

IN THE FACE OF HOSTILITY

LUKE 5:17-26

People heard that Jesus was back in town from the wilderness, and they packed out Peter's house to hear Him teach.

Mixed in with the listeners, that day, were several religious authorities who were always hounding Jesus. They were trying to catch Him saying, or doing, something against their law.

> **LEADERSHIP TIP #40**
>
> Defeat intimidation from your opponents by being a conduit of God's touch to others.

While Jesus was speaking, four men were carrying their paralyzed friend on a stretcher to the house. They were hoping Jesus would heal him. However, they got there too late, and they couldn't get in. So, using some creativity, they carried their friend on the stretcher up the outside stairs to the roof. They first found where they could hear Jesus speaking directly below them. Next, they rapidly started taking the roof apart, tile by tile. Jesus stopped talking, and watched.

Finally, they lowered their friend through the hole, down in front of Jesus. Then, in spite of threatening stares from the religious leaders, Jesus told the man, "Your sins are forgiven." He knew that would get a reaction. He was right.

> How can keeping in mind you are a conduit for God help you defeat the attempted intimidation of others?

VISIBLE PROVES INVISIBLE

LUKE 5:17-26

As soon as Jesus told the paralyzed man his sins were forgiven, the religious leaders started whispering among themselves. Jesus saw it, and
He quickly took the at-
tack to them. He asked
"Which is easier to say,
'your sins are forgiven,'
or 'get up and walk?'"

LEADERSHIP TIP #41

Consistently backing your word with
results will help your people take
you at your word in other projects,
before you can produce results.

Clearly, it was easier to
say, "your sins are forgiven." There was no way to prove it.
Yet, even the religious authorities knew only God could do
both. Jesus quickly added, "So that you will know the Son
of Man has the authority on earth to forgive sins…" Then, a
pause. And, perhaps kneeling in front of the paralytic, He continued: "I tell you, get up, take your mat, and go home.'"

The townspeople, who were crammed into the house, stretched
their necks, trying to see what would happen. Four men peered
down expectantly through the immense hole. And, the defiant
religious leaders just shook their heads in disgust. Then the
man did exactly what Jesus told him to do.

He got up.

What projects can you instruct your people to do that will increase their
confidence in you?

TREATING SOMEONE AS A "TEN"

LUKE 5:27-28

Not long after Jesus had healed the paralytic, He was walking along a busy road near the lake with His followers. They were approaching a tax-stand operated by a Jewish tax-collector, named Levi.

LEADERSHIP TIP #42

Treat people as a "10" in spite of their actions, words, attitudes, and how other people treat them.

Now, tax-collectors were hated by the Jewish people, and here's why. Jewish tax-collectors worked for the Roman government. Yet, they collected taxes from their own people. And, not only collected, but they charged them huge rates in stuffing their own money bags. To the people, the word, "sinner," could be defined by two words, "tax-collector."

Jesus and His followers stopped in front of Levi's booth. Then, as His men gathered round the front of the stand, Jesus fixed His eyes on Levi. In fact, He looked into the very heart of the hated man. Jesus' entourage could only see Levi for how he had ripped them off. On a rating scale of 1 to 10, they would have given him a minus-three. That's how they treated him. Jesus saw Levi as a ten. That's how He treated him.

1. How would you, in detail, describe a "10" on a ten-point scale?

2. What three things can you do to treat each of the people you're leading as a "10"?

SEEING POTENTIAL IN A REJECT

LUKE 5:27-28

God helped Jesus to look into the very heart of Levi and see his potential. Others standing next to Jesus, on their own, could only see Levi for what they perceived him to be. A self-absorbed, money-loving, rip-off artist. Most likely, every one of Jesus' men wanted

LEADERSHIP TIP #43

Ask God to help you look beyond the surface of others, to their potential.

Him to turn away from Levi, and move on.

Peter and the rest of Jesus' followers must have had to pick their jaws up off the ground. They couldn't have been less prepared for what they heard Jesus say. Levi was caught off guard, too. They were the same two words Jesus' disciples had heard Jesus, at an earlier time, speak to each of them. "Follow me," He invited Levi to do, looking into his eyes.

Now, why did Jesus recruit such a reject as Levi? Because He knew who Levi could become. And, He knew what would happen as a result of who he would become. Levi, by the way, was another name for Matthew. He was one of only four people God chose to write the official story of Jesus. With Jesus' help, the hated tax-collector lived up to the potential Jesus saw in him.

What qualities do you feel God would have you look for in other people, and how would you see them?

A Banquet of Outcasts

LUKE 5:29-32

Levi was so enthused about the challenge of following Jesus, he threw a party. He wanted all of his friends to meet his new "boss." Jesus, of course, was also eager to meet Levi's friends. They were a mixture of other tax-collectors and, most likely, more outcasts of society.

LEADERSHIP TIP #44

Reach out to people of all backgrounds and social levels in bringing them touches of God's love.

Some religious top dogs passing by the festivities asked some of the disciples, "Why do you eat with tax-collectors, and other scum?" They thought any person of spiritual uprightness would be above that. Perhaps a disciple reported to Jesus what one of the religious leaders had asked. Or, maybe, Jesus just overheard the question.

Either way, Jesus quickly walked over to the "holier-than-thou" leaders. He got right to the point. "It is not the healthy who need a doctor," He said, "but the sick. I have not come to call the righteous, but sinners to repentance." Jesus felt right at home with Levi's friends. Why? Because He knew His Father designed each of them, loved them, and Jesus wanted to recruit each of them into His Father's Forever Kingdom.

How can you direct your organization to reach out to people in all walks of life?

ON THE ROAD
WITH JESUS

Year Two

DEDICATED TO
REBECCA DUNCAN

This section is in honor of my oldest daughter, my first pride and joy, who I still brag to others she was walking at six months of age. The best I can figure, Rebecca, you haven't stopped keeping a hectic pace since that proud day. I still don't know how you do it. It must be in the genes. On your mom's side, that is.

In this section, we move into our second year with Jesus. During this eventful year, Jesus teaches His leadership team many practical rights and wrongs of life, and begins to mold them together as a family, albeit a bit dysfunctional. We also will "be in the boat" with Jesus when He calms a raging storm, and finally "be there" as He and Peter walk on water. At least, Peter did for a few steps.

Rebecca, from the very beginning, you have had a sharp eye for what's right, and what's wrong, and you're not afraid to stand for the "right." Wow! Talk about "calming storms." Raising three energetic kids is not easy for anyone. But, yours have that extra energy, just like you had at their age. You are the best "storm calmer." Also, you're not afraid to get out of the boat, and move toward what God has called you to do. You're a chip off the old block. Okay, so you're really the "block." I don't mind being the "chip." Rebecca, my day is always made when I hear my cell phone ring, and on the other end, "Hi, Dad." Yes, without a doubt, you light up my day!

Grain on the Sabbath

Mark 2:23-28

It was a Sabbath after Levi's banquet. Jesus and His men were walking along the outer rows of a grainfield when His men picked some heads of grain to eat. That, in itself, was all right. In fact, farmers planted the outer rows so travelers could pick the grain to satisfy their hunger.

> **LEADERSHIP TIP #45**
>
> Put the needs of people ahead of even the age-old traditions of your organization.

However, the religious people, who were hounding Jesus and His men, finally had a charge against Him. The disciples had picked the grain on the Sabbath. Absolutely no work was allowed on that holy day. Picking grain, and rubbing it together to get rid of the hulls, was thought of as work. Sure, that was nit-picking, but the religious "nit-pickers" were looking for anything to find fault in Jesus. What the disciples did, would do.

Jesus took it right back to them. He noted that even the widely admired King David made a religious exception. While David was on the run and hungry, he had eaten bread that, according to Jewish law, only priests could eat. Jesus then added, "The Sabbath was made for man, not man for the Sabbath."

> What policies, or traditions, might need changing in your organization to better serve your people?

ASKING QUESTIONS

MARK 3:1-6

After the grain-field confrontation, the religious hierarchy had figured out a way to catch Jesus defiling the Sabbath. They knew a man with a shriveled hand would be in the synagogue the day Jesus would be there. They also figured Jesus would have compassion on the man, and heal him.

> **LEADERSHIP TIP #46**
>
> Ask thought-provoking questions to take the offense away from someone who is trying to keep you from doing what God has called you to do.

Of course, that would be a no-no. Healing on the Sabbath was considered work. Even medical doctors were not allowed to help anyone get better on the Sabbath. So, if Jesus healed the man, the leaders could bring charges against Him. The trap was set. It was ready to spring.

Jesus looked direcly at the man. Then He looked angrily at the religious leaders in the front rows. He knew what they were up to. In defiance of them, Jesus motioned to the man. "Stand up here," He called out. As the man got to his feet, Jesus turned back to the leaders, "Which is lawful on the Sabbath," He asked, "to do good, or to do evil, to save life or to kill?" The people were on Jesus' side. So much for the trap.

> What can you ask a person who tries to prevent you from doing what you know you need to do?

Enemies Unite Against Jesus

MARK 3:1-6

The man with the shriveled hand walked up to the front of the synagogue, next to Jesus. Sitting in front, the religious leaders couldn't believe that Jesus was actually going to do it in total defiance of them. It was humiliating.

LEADERSHIP TIP #47

People who don't normally get along with each other might unite in a joint effort against you.

Then the carpenter from Nazareth looked into the man's hopeful eyes. And, perhaps with a smile and a nod of his head, He told the man, "Stretch out your hand."

Before the amazed eyes of all the people, God helped the man do exactly that. His crooked fingers stretched out all the way. Each of them was completely straight. Jesus healed the man right in front of the high and mighty "spiritual" top dogs.

Well, the Pharisees were fuming. Jesus had put it to them in the presence of a packed-out synagogue. Abruptly, each one of the officials rose to his feet, and stormed out of the building. They quickly looked for, and found, their arch enemies, the Herodians. Enemies, yes. But, now, partners in trying to put a stop to Jesus. If fact, in trying to kill Him.

If Jesus knew His act of kindness could possibly cause Him problems down the road, why did He heal the man?

67

PRAYING FOR MULTIPLICATION

LUKE 6:12-16

After the latest synagogue conflict, Jesus' reputation was spreading like wildfire. Mainly, throughout Galilee. So, whenever He visited different villages, large crowds gathered to hear Him.

LEADERSHIP TIP #48

Spend time in concentrated prayer before choosing people through whom you will multiply yourself.

Now, a more committed bunch of people, had also been trailing along with Him from town to town. They were sticking with Him wherever He went. In fact, they couldn't get enough of Him. He spoke to their hearts, as well as their minds.

One afternoon, Jesus left His followers at the base of a mountain. He then hiked up the side to spend the entire night in prayer. Why such a long and intense time in prayer? His Father had impressed Him to choose a smaller group of men. Men into whom He could pour Himself over a period of time.

Jesus was thinking in terms of multiplication. He knew it would be the few who would eventually take His message to the world. But, who would those few be? Concentrated prayer was the only way that even Jesus could be sure He had His Father's leading.

Why is it important to multiply yourself, and what can that mean to your work?

THE LEADERSHIP TEAM

LUKE 6:12-16

As Jesus prayed the entire night, His Father let Him know who to pick for His team. So, when He hiked down the mountain, He made His selection. Jesus "singled" out twelve men, none of whom would stand out in a crowd. None of whom would make any "Who's Who" list. Unless, of course, it was for the most common people of the land. Yet, in each of them, God helped Jesus see their potential. Whether each man would live up to that potential was still in question. Only time would tell. But, for the present, Jesus selected men who would be teachable, and who appeared to line up with His values.

> **LEADERSHIP TIP #49**
>
> Select only people for your leadership group who are teachable, and who are committed to line up with your values.

Among them were four uneducated fishermen, a hated tax-collector, a skeptic, the hot-tempered, and the politically zealous. Quite a mixture of opposites. Not the making of a winning team. Yet, even with a future traitor, that team of misfits would eventually take His message to the world. And, each of them, except for the traitor, would be willing to die for Jesus. Quite a team, after all.

> How will you determine if a person is teachable, and will line up with your values?

69

Training is the Key

LUKE 6:12-16

Why did Jesus form a smaller group of followers, an "elite" group for special training? Sure, it was because His Father impressed Him to do so. But, why? It might be easier to understand when we understand how God works in the world.

> **LEADERSHIP TIP #50**
>
> Multiply your efforts through the training of others.

God has always worked through His creation. That means working through both nature and people. It was in a person that God was making Himself fully known. Through Jesus. So, it was inevitable that God would direct His Son to choose other people. People who would be conduits through whom He would take His love to the entire world.

Jesus planned for His team to multiply His efforts. And, after training those men, He intended for them, in turn, to train still other "multipliers." They would eventually have to be able to sense what He Himself would do in any situation. How? By getting to know Him, and being in partnership with Him. The key is in training.

1. How do you think having a solid team of committed people will enhance what God has called you to do?

2. What program do you have, or will develop, that will keep training your team to be more effective?

70

A Time of Training

MATTHEW 5 – 7

We don't know for sure if Jesus gave His famous Sermon on the Mount all at the same time, or not. Matthew might have collected many of Jesus' teachings and lumped them all together. However, we do know that all of the teachings are directly from Jesus. That isn't seriously in question.

LEADERSHIP TIP #51

Train your people in specific areas of conduct.

In this playbook, we'll be taking the teachings in the exact order that Matthew recorded them. So, let's assume, for the sake of flow, that Jesus did give all of these teachings at one time.

One day, as a crowd was gathering around Jesus, He led His newly selected team up on a mountainside. Then, sitting down on the grassy slope with everyone, He began to teach. His purpose was to give the people brief lessons on what life would be like in His Father's Kingdom. Lessons also on how they ought to be living their lives right then and there.

Jesus Himself was the perfect model for each lesson. That's also something He called His followers to be. Models for the values they were to pass on to others.

What steps do you need to take to improve the training of the people you lead?

CASTING THE VISION

MATTHEW 5 – 7

Jesus had so much to tell His eager listeners. Yet, He knew they wouldn't be able to take it all in. It just wouldn't be possible. No one could remember everything He wanted to share with them. At least, in hearing it only once.

> ### LEADERSHIP TIP #52
>
> Keep in front of your people a picture of what the future will be like to help motivate them to a higher standard of conduct.

However, in the next hour, or so, Jesus would give all the people, especially His own team, a vision. He knew that people performed better when they had a clear vision in mind. When they knew where they were going.

His vision was of His Father's Kingdom. Not only the Kingdom in this present world, but also in the world to come. A vision of what His team would see Him model before their eyes in the years to come. A vision of what He was calling them to also be, and do.

It would be a vision of an exciting New World. A world His followers could eagerly recruit other people to join with them in living forever with each other, and with Him.

1. What standard of conduct do you want for the people you're leading?

2. What vision will you give to your people to help keep your code of conduct in front of them?

THE POOR IN SPIRIT

MATTHEW 5:3

Jesus started His message about living in the New World by talking about the "poor in spirit." He used that term in describing a person who has come to the end of himself. A person who is totally empty of ego and pride. Simply put, it's someone who recognizes his need for God.

> **LEADERSHIP TIP #53**
>
> By being empty of yourself, and tuned into God, you will experience all that God has for you now, and in eternity.

What does Jesus promise an empty-of-self person? He guarantees a blessing. In fact, the Greek word Jesus used for "blessed" in these first few teachings of His vision, is the highest form of happiness. Jesus said the one who recognizes his need for God, couldn't possibly be any happier when God gives him the reward.

Now, here's the amazing reward. To such an "empty" person, one who is one hundred percent tuned into God, God will give His entire kingdom. That's right. His entire Kingdom. That person will totally experience God, and all the pleasure and contentment that comes from walking with God. Jesus taught the key to being full of God was, first, to be empty of self.

> How can you be "empty" of yourself, and tuned into God, when the world all around shouts out to elevate yourself?

73

Those Who Mourn

Matthew 5:4

Jesus then told the crowd, "God blesses those who mourn, for they will be comforted." The word Jesus used in this teaching for "mourn" is not just being sad. It's the most intense form of sorrow. It's the anguish that would be ripping you apart if something terrible happened to the one you loved the most. Your heart would be broken into a million pieces. Shattered like a fragile, crystal vase falling on a cement slab.

> **LEADERSHIP TIP #54**
>
> Be intensely sorry for your own thoughts, attitudes, and actions that fall short of God, and He will give you His comfort.

The word includes your sorrow for what has happened to others. However, here's the twist. Its most direct meaning, in this teaching, is your intense sadness because of *your own* thoughts, attitudes and actions that are apart from God.

Jesus promised those who experience this mourning, God's "salve" through the mental and spiritual relief He will personally give. He will exchange your gnawing pain for His calmness and peace.

> 1. As you take inventory of your thoughts, attitudes and actions, how do you feel about them, and how do you think God feels about them?
>
> 2. How can you pass this same blessing on to others you lead who have blown it badly with you?

THE GENTLE

MATTHEW 5:5

"God blesses those who are gentle and lowly," Jesus continued, "for the whole earth will belong to them." Now, don't be misled. Jesus' use of the word "gentle" in this teaching does not imply a softness. In fact, it's just the opposite. The word actually means a toughness and a great strength

LEADERSHIP TIP #55

Reward, with increased privileges, those you lead who exhibit a control of their anger,

in controlling one's anger. The word carries with it the picture of a strong horse being broken in such a way he will obey his master's commands. How? Through a simple tug on the reins. The horse's strength is still there. It's just controlled.

Jesus used this word "gentle" to describe a person who was completely God-controlled. Now, talk about rewards. What could be greater than to inherit the earth? Nothing shabby about that. In other words, to such a God-controlled person, the new earth will one day belong. Yes, one day, God will resurrect this present earth into a new earth (2 Peter 3:13 and Revelation 21:1). And, on that new earth, Jesus said, His "gentle" followers, with Him, will have the run of the place.

1. What can you imagine your enjoyment on the new earth will be like?

2. What privileges can you give to those who consistently demonstrate a controlling of their anger?

CRAVING GOD'S WAY

MATTHEW 5:6

Jesus knew the world would keep changing its standard for right and wrong. He also knew, in His own land, that, what was "right" in one culture was "wrong" in another.

LEADERSHIP TIP #56

Help those you lead develop a craving for God's values and His ways.

However, in this teaching, Jesus gave the highest standard for doing right, a standard that would pass the test in any culture.

His standard for righteousness, or justice, was God Himself. He said, "God blesses those who hunger and thirst for righteousness, for they will be filled." Now, the word He used for "hunger" describes a person who has the deepest, gnawing hunger pangs. So, when Jesus was talking about hungering and thirsting for "righteousness," He was describing a person with deep cravings for doing things God's way.

Jesus taught that a person who hungered and thirsted after God's right way of doing things would be rewarded. What reward? God will bring that person the satisfaction in this present world to match the person's craving for His ways.

1. What cravings for God's ways do you personally have?

2. How can you help those you lead to also crave for God's way of doing things?

THE MERCIFUL

MATTHEW 5:7

Next, in His rapid-fire delivery, Jesus said, "God blesses those who are merciful, for they will be shown mercy." "Mercy" as Jesus used it in this teaching is not just having pity on someone. It is that, but it goes far deeper.

LEADERSHIP TIP #57

Have "getting into the skin" kind of mercy for all the people you lead, including your own family.

Having mercy implies getting into another person's skin, seeing the situation through that person's eyes. It means feeling about what's going on in that person's life the same way that person feels about it. It's having total empathy, crawling into the other person's mind.

Interestingly, God's reward for a person having that kind of mercy is to get the same kind of mercy when they need it. Now, keep in mind God works His ways through people. So, as you're "getting into the skin" of someone else, and feeling what they're feeling, God Himself is touching that person through you. Likewise, Jesus said, when you need a dose of mercy, God will work through someone else to touch you. That's His promise.

1. What can you do to be more sensitive to the needs of the people you lead?

2. How can you train your people to have this same kind of empathy for their fellow workers, and the people they serve?

The Pure in Heart

MATTHEW 5:8

Who doesn't want to see God, or, at least hear from Him? Well, Jesus knew that's exactly what was on His followers minds. They all wanted to connect with God. That's why they had followed Him up the mountain. So, as Jesus stood in front of His listeners, He said, "God blesses those whose hearts are pure. They will see Him."

> **LEADERSHIP TIP #58**
>
> See God's activity by looking at every moment through the eyes of Jesus.

"Pure," as Jesus used the word, means to be unpolluted from anything that doesn't line up with God's values. It includes thoughts, attitudes, and actions that are not mixed together with ungodly things.

Now, here's what Jesus said is the "pure-in-heart" person's reward. He will "see" God. No, not physically, since God isn't physical. This word for "see" does not imply physical vision. It means mental perception, or full understanding. So, as a person keeps his mind free of ungodly influences, God will help that person more fully understand Him. Or, "see" Him.

1. How can you use the Bible to help you be pure?

2. What can you do to help those you lead develop pure thoughts, attitudes, actions and motives?

THE PEACEMAKERS

MATTHEW 5:9

Jesus' next teaching dug deep into the hearts of His team of misfits, men who were often at odds with each other. "God blesses the peacemakers," He taught, "for they will be called childeren of God."

Being a "peacemaker," as Jesus used the term, is

> **LEADERSHIP TIP #59**
>
> Look for ways you can help conflicting people see the situation from the other person's viewpoint.

a tough job. It's hard enough to keep the peace. It's even more difficult to bring about peace in the middle of tensions. The word "peacemaker" describes a person who actually goes out of his way to bring conflicting people together. Out of his way, mind you. It means helping each person see the situation from the other person's viewpoint.

Peacemaking is a tough assignment that Jesus gave His followers. But, what a great reward. Such a person, one who actively gets involved in helping people resolve their differences, will be called a child of God. Okay, so why is that such a big deal? Because it means, if you are being a peacemaker, you are caught up in what God is doing. Can you think of anything greater than partnering with God in His activity?

1. What people in your world of influence are at odds with each other?

2. How might God use you to be a peacemaker?

RELENTLESS OPPOSITION

MATTHEW 5:10-12

On that sunny hillside dotted with wildflowers, everything looked so peaceful. So, Jesus' next lesson must have shocked His men. He talked about persecution. "God blesses those who are persecuted because they live for God." His point?

> **LEADERSHIP TIP #60**
>
> Keep a vision of rewards in front of those you lead to help them get through tough projects. Then, make sure you deliver on those rewards.

Satan is active, and he is in direct opposition to God. Satan has set up a system in this world to oppose anyone who is a "God-lover." Anyone who is a follower of Jesus. So, as Jesus' followers are committed to honor God, Jesus warned them. They will face relentless opposition. Expect it. It has happened to people down through the centuries.

However, as Jesus said, "The Kingdom of Heaven is theirs." His followers will gain eternal life in the Kingdom of Heaven itself. A quality of life far beyond anything experienced in this present world. Jesus would constantly keep that vision of the coming world in front of His followers. A mental picture of a future certainty.

> 1. What reward/s can you give for current projects?
>
> 2. How can you keep a vision of your rewards in front of the people you lead?

THE FLAVOR OF GOD

Matthew 5:13

"You are the salt of the earth." What a description Jesus just gave His followers. They knew salt provided flavor for food, and it was used as a preservative. However, they also knew salt was a symbol for purity.

LEADERSHIP TIP #61

Add the flavor of God and His values to the product or service you provide.

Jesus wanted His followers to know that each of them was called to be pure in God's ways. To preserve God's way of doing things. On top of that, each follower was also charged to add the flavor of God to the life of others.

Jesus gave His followers more than just a description of who God wanted them to be. He also warned them of what would happen if they didn't take their role in this world seriously.

God would consider them as worthless, in building God's kingdom, as salt that has lost its flavor. It was common to see piles of salt tossed out on the ground because it had lost its flavor...lost its effectiveness.

Jesus' warning for His followers? Be the flavor of God to others. Don't become like salt that's tossed away as useless, and of no value. Be the salt that's chock full of flavor!

How will you add God's flavor to your product or service?

81

LIGHTING UP THE WORLD

MATTHEW 5:14-16

Jesus might have paused for a moment, looking around at His listeners, basking in the sunlight. Then He told them "You are the light of the world." However, later, Jesus would call Himself the "light of the world" (John 8:12).

LEADERSHIP TIP #62

See yourself as a vehicle through which Jesus will shine out to the people you lead.

Now, in the Greek language, there are several words for "light." One describes a light resulting from its own source, like the sun. Another describes a light that reflects light from another source, like the moon.

When Jesus called Himself the "light," He used the word for light resulting from its own source, like the sun. Surprisingly, Jesus didn't use the word for reflective light to describe His followers. Instead, He used the same word He used to describe Himself. So, wouldn't a follower of Jesus have to be a light that reflects the light of Jesus? How can he be a light from his own source? The only way is for Jesus to be living in and through His followers. He Himself is their light.

1. What can you do to become a more pure vehicle for Jesus to shine through to the people you lead?

2. In what ways, can Jesus shine through you?

GREATNESS

MATTHEW 5:19

Jesus knew that most people want to know their life is counting for something in this world. As He looked out over His listeners, He knew each of them had that same longing. "Anyone who obeys God's laws," He said, "and teaches them will be great in the Kingdom." In this teaching

> **LEADERSHIP TIP #63**
>
> Personally practice and teach the people you lead God's values, and His ways.

about greatness, Jesus didn't mention physical accomplishments, things like building cities, or giving away millions of dollars. That's how the world describes greatness. Instead, Jesus told His people that greatness was teaching other people God's values, and His way of doing things.

Come on, what's so great about that? Why does Jesus underline that greatness is helping others learn God's values and His ways? Well, psychologists tell us that what's in our mind dictates our actions. That's how God has designed us. So, if we have God's values in our mind, we will do those things that line up with His values. "Doing" is an extension of our mind. And, nothing is greater than doing things God's way, in close fellowship with Him. Jesus felt that was greatness.

> What are three values of God you will help instill in those you lead, and why did you select the values you did?

Controlling Anger

MATTHEW 5:22

Jesus' listeners were well-versed in the Scriptures, those that we now call the Old Testament. It was with this next nugget-lesson that Jesus started contrasting His teachings with what was taught in those Scriptures.

> **LEADERSHIP TIP #64**
>
> Instead of allowing yourself to get angry, ask God to help you see the situation as He does.

Now, Jesus, in no way, was lessening the value of the Old Testament teachings. They were from God, and He Himself lived by them. However, starting with this instruction, Jesus took the "old" teachings to a new and higher level. He began to define what purity truly was in God's eyes. A purity Jesus was calling His followers to in an impure world.

He said it wasn't enough just "not" to murder someone, as the old Scriptures taught. "If you are even angry with someone," He explained, "you deserve a sentence from God."

Jesus was calling His followers to control their anger. Not "just" to keep from murdering someone, as important as that was.

1. Jesus got angry in the temple. So, what's the difference between His anger in the temple and the anger we have most of the time?

2. How will you control your anger, and help those you lead control their anger?

RECONCILIATION

MATTHEW 5:23-24

Jesus wanted His followers to be at peace with others. Not just with other believers, but also with those who weren't following Him. He told them, "So if you are presenting a sacrifice at the altar in the Temple and you suddenly remember that someone has something against you, leave your

> **LEADERSHIP TIP #65**
>
> As a first step in resolving a conflict, ask God to help you see the situation from that person's viewpoint.

sacrifice there at the altar. Go and be reconciled to that person. Then come and offer your sacrifice to God."

The word "reconciled" implies the first person chooses to see the situation through the eyes of the second person. Doesn't have to agree with him. Just see it the way the other person does. That helps cause the second person to see the situation through the eyes of the first person.

Jesus also put the word "reconciled" in the passive voice. That means reconciliation is something that happens to you and the other person. You don't make it happen. God causes a change in feelings when the two people are committed to see the situation from the other person's viewpoint. How can that possibly happen? By asking God to make it happen.

> How can you train the people you lead to reconcile with others in their life?

Friends With Opponents

Matthew 5:25-26

Perhaps with some acting out, Jesus gave His hillside audience a mental picture. It was of a person being dragged off to court, then being put into jail, because of a problem with another person.

His message to His followers? "When you are on the way to court with your adversary, settle your differences quick-

> ## LEADERSHIP TIP #66
>
> As long as it's still is in your hands, make friends with a person who has brought charges against you, and work at resolving the matter out of court.

ly." Now, why get things sorted out with someone before they even get you to court? Jesus' idea was that, once in court, you would be in the hands of the judicial system. It would be out of your own hands.

This teaching ties in beautifully with what Jesus had just taught the crowd about reconciliation. However, in this instruction, Jesus took it beyond just changing one's attitude toward another. He told His people to take specific actions that would help resolve the problem. The central point is, whether it's just a change of feelings, or a series of actions that need to be taken, the resolution would still be in the hands of the individuals, not in the court system.

How is it possible to make friends with someone who has brought charges against you?

Dealing With Lust

Matthew 5:27-28

Jesus knew that lust could either be good or bad. The word simply means to fix one's desires on something, and to direct one's affections toward that something.

LEADERSHIP TIP #67

Keep yourself from lusting after another person by intensely focusing on something else at that time.

So, if we're lusting after God and His ways, that's a good lust. Jesus wanted His followers to lust after God. However, in Jesus' next teaching, He was talking about a bad kind of lust. He said, "Anyone who even looks at a woman with lust has already committed adultery with her in his heart." Now, here's the kind of lust Jesus is talking about. It's taking an attraction for another person to the corrupting level of mentally having sexual activity with that person.

In God's eyes, Jesus equated mental adultery with actually committing physical adultery. So, why is lusting that bad? At least three reasons. It takes us away from God's best at that moment. It can lead us to ungodly actions. And, it deadens our sensitivity to God.

---

1. Why does God equate mental sexual activity with physical sexual activity?.

2. How can mental sexual activty influence how you think of, and treat, people of the opposite sex?

Removing the Cause of Sin

MATTHEW 5:29-30

Maybe lust wasn't a problem for everyone in the crowd. How-ever, everyone knew they were a sinner. Who didn't miss the mark of God's perfec-tion? So, they must have sat straight up on the grassy slope when Jesus gave them the remedy for their sin problem. "If your hand, even your stronger hand, causes

LEADERSHIP TIP #68

Remove, or change, whatever is necessary in order to keep you from having thoughts, and taking actions, apart form God.

you to sin, cut it off and throw it away." Now, that sounds kind of drastic, doesn't it? Did Jesus really mean for them to mutilate themselves?

Well, yes and no. You see, Jesus was using the hand to get across how absolutely necessary it was for His followers to deal with sin in their lives. He knew our eyes and hands don't really cause us to sin. They simply carry out the directions of our mind. Jesus was telling His followers "cut it off" to make a major point. Here it is: Remove whatever is causing you to think in a way that will lead to actions apart from God's best for your life.

1. What steps will you take to have a more godly mind?

2. What might you need to change in your place of work to help the people you lead be more pure in their thinking?

Only Grounds for Divorce

Matthew 5:31-32

Jesus seemed to be in the groove for more hard hitting. His next teaching had to do with the tight bond of marriage in God's eyes. "A man who divorces his wife," He sais, "unless she has been unfaithful, causes her to commit adultery."

> **LEADERSHIP TIP #69**
>
> Counsel the people you lead to ask God to help them work out their marital problems.

Jesus taught His followers the only valid grounds for divorce was adultery. Not mental cruelty. Not irreconcilable differences. Adultery, and only adultery. Why just adultery? Probably because all other problems in marriage can, in time, be worked out. However, adultery actually physically links the spouse to another person. That can never be undone. Forgiven yes, but not undone.

Jesus was not saying that adultery should lead to divorce. He only meant that adultery was the only grounds, in God's eyes, for the splitting up of a husband and wife. Keep in mind that, like any other sin, God will forgive. If the person, or people, involved go to Him with a genuinely remorseful and repentant heart, He will forgive. God can, and will, give the repentant person a fresh start.

> In what way *might* the term "adultery" include other severe problems, such as being married to a person who has become homicidal, or who is addicted to pornography and refuses help?

A LIFETIME COMMITMENT

MATTHEW 5:31-32

Jesus didn't stop with just teaching His followers that adultery was the only grounds for divorce. He continued to explain how important this issue was to God. He said that a woman who was divorced for anything other than adultery would be committing adultery if she remarried. Jesus then added another ingredient to the divorce recipe.

> **LEADERSHIP TIP #70**
>
> Encourage the people you lead to receive in-depth biblical training on marriage, and raising children.

He raised a few eyebrows when He said, "Anyone who marries a divorced woman also commits adultery." Now, that might not have seemed so tough for Jesus' day. Divorce wasn't that big of an issue. However, in our present day permissive society, that's a pretty harsh teaching. Yet, in God's sight, it's still true. Remember, God doesn't change (James 1:17).

So, why is marriage so important to God? Mainly, because He designed the family to model His kingdom for the world, His way of doing things. If Christian marriages fall apart, where does the world go for a model of God's values?

1. How can you help the people you lead understand God's values of marriage, and why He is so strong on the issue of divorce?

2. What steps will you take to implement your program about God's view of marriage?

GIVING YOUR WORD

MATTHEW 5:33-37

Jesus was a man of His word, and He taught His followers to be the same. He said, "Just say a simple, 'Yes, I will,' or 'No, I won't.'" What's His point? A person's word was enough. He should not have to back it up with anything but action.

LEADERSHIP TIP #71

Follow through with whatever you say you'll do as an expression of your loyalty to Jesus.

Of course, Jesus knew that some of His listeners did have a problem with keeping their word. Not that they didn't want to. And, not that they didn't mean what they said when they said it. It was just they would get so caught up in other things. They would either forget what they said, or they would just run out of time to follow through with action. What they promised would get lost in an avalanche of other things to do.

Now, in this teaching, Jesus was talking to all of His followers. Not just the more disciplined ones. He wanted all of His people to follow through on what they promised. Why? Because giving one's word was a reflection of one's loyalty to God. Just as Jesus' words and actions illustrated His commitment to His Father.

How does following through, or not following through, after giving your word, reflect on your loyalty to Jesus?

91

TURNING THE OTHER CHEEK

MATTHEW 5:38-41

On the slope that day, Jesus' listeners had never heard any more revolutionary teachings than those He was giving them. They were life-changing. His instruction on taking revenge was no different.

LEADERSHIP TIP #72

Give a blessing to a person who has purposely hurt you, instead of seeking revenge.

Now, what God implemented in the Old Testament -- the practice of an eye for an eye, and a tooth for a tooth -- was a punishment equal to the crime. Nevertheless, in ushering in the new kingdom, Jesus taught a new way.

Jesus told His followers to turn the other cheek, and to go the extra mile. What a shock it was for the person who slugged a follower of Jesus. He got another cheek to hit. What a surprise it was for the Roman soldier, who demanded a Christian to carry his gear for one mile. The carrier would insist on hauling it even further. Jesus wanted the conduct of His followers to speak louder than their words alone.

He knew that people would pay more attention to His followers' words when they saw the integrity of their hearts spelled out in their actions.

How will Jesus' teaching on "turning the other cheek" work? Won't people take advantage of such passive behavior? Or, is it passive?

Lending and Giving

Matthew 5:42

People in Jesus' audience knew not to loan money to someone who wouldn't be able to pay it back. So, everyone in the crowd, including His disciples, must have been surpised at what Jesus said next.

> **LEADERSHIP TIP #73**
>
> Supply the need of someone who asks for, or wants to borrow, something you have without expecting anything in return.

"Give to those who ask, and don't turn away from those who want to borrow." Was Jesus actually teaching to lend to anyone who asked? Yes, that's exactly what He said. Even if they can't pay it back? Yes, even if they can't pay it back. Wow! What a sure-fire way to go broke. Or, is it?

What does it all mean?

It means, even though we can't forsee how God will do it, He is committed to make it work. True, this new teaching about lending to anyone who asks doesn't make a lot of sense in today's world. But, it is God's way.

1. How would you handle it if many of the people you lead come to you for a loan, and your resources are not enough to take care of them all?

2. How can you train your people to be charitable with their resources in this manner, or is this teaching only for followers of Jesus?

How to Treat Enemies

MATTHEW 5:43-47

Jesus' new teachings were almost always opposite of His listener's natural leanings. It was easy for them to be kind to people who treated them kindly. But, how were they at being kind to someone who was out to get them?

LEADERSHIP TIP #74

Ask Jesus to love your enemies through you, and make them your friends.

Well, that's exactly what Jesus instructed His followers to do: "You have heard the law that says, 'Love your neighbor' and hate your enemy. But I say, love your enemies! Pray for those who persecute you!" To love their enemies. To actually love them. How was that even possible? Only one way.

Jesus knew His followers would be able to love their enemies only as they allowed Him to love their enemies through them. Now, Jesus' kind of love wasn't some syrupy emotion. It was an intentional choice for His followers to make. To ask Him to help them put the best interests of someone else ahead of their own. Yes, Jesus said, even their enemies.

1. Why does Jesus want His followers to love their enemies?

2. How can you train your people to love even those people who give them a hard time?

Praying for Enemies

MATTHEW 5:43-47

The inner circle of Jesus' followers already knew how much importance their leader put on prayer. They not only had often listened in when He was praying. They also saw Him "disappear" to isolated places for more concentrated times of talking with His Father.

> ## LEADERSHIP TIP #75
>
> Pray that God will bless those who are actively working against you.

They saw in Jesus a man who believed that prayer moved God to do what God wanted to do, but wouldn't do without a person praying. Jesus taught it. And, He did it...throughout the day, consistently.

However, His close friends had to be surprised when their mentor took prayer to another level. When He directed them to pray even for people who were being cruel to them. That's right. To pray God would even bless people against them.

Here's how Jesus saw it. Praying for good things to happen for another person was the best, and most effective, action anyone could take on behalf of someone else. Jesus was actually ordering His followers to do this for people who were against them. It sure didn't make sense. Or, did it?

1. How does prayer actually work?

2. Why does Jesus want you to pray for people who are against you?

95

BEING LIKE GOD

MATTHEW 5:48

"You are to be perfect, even as your Father in heaven is perfect." The people were scratching their heads on that one. *Can He really be serious?* they must have wondered. *How can anyone be perfect like God? Is that even possible?*

> **LEADERSHIP TIP #76**
>
> Use God's way of doing things, as revealed through Jesus and the Bible, as your only standard as a leader.

Well, it certainly wasn't for Peter. His brother, Andrew, could tell Jesus that. And, Philip wasn't the picture of perfection either. His good friend, Nathanael, could vouch for that. So, what did Jesus really mean when He told His disciples to be perfect? Did He mean they were to be absolutely flawless, like God? Without any blemish at all?

Jesus knew His followers would never be 100% perfect like God. That wasn't His point. His point was that God was the only standard for the right way of doing things. Since that was true, Jesus was commanding His followers to zero in on God's way, and no other way. Only Jesus was perfect like His Father. His follower's responsibility was to learn from Him the ways of God. Then, allow Him to help them do it God's way.

> What practical steps will you take to line up your entire work with the teachings of Jesus?

Rewards for Pure Giving

Matthew 6:3-4

Right after Jesus puzzled His audience by telling them they should be perfect like God was perfect, He talked about rewards. He told His listeners God actually rewarded people who did things His way. "Give your gifts in secret," He said, and your Father, who sees everything, will reward

> ### LEADERSHIP TIP #77
>
> Give out of a pure and sincere heart, and God will reward you in His way and in His timing.

you." The truth is, God is the originator of the reward system. Why? Because He knew it would work.

Jesus also knew it was only natural for people to want something in return for what they did. In fact, if some people didn't get acclaim for what they did, Jesus knew they wouldn't even do it. Now, that "wanting credit" was true for His disciples in giving, as well. However, Jesus taught His followers that giving to others for public applause wasn't God's way. The only "applause" His people would need is from God. And, God would give it only for people who gave out of pure motives.

> 1. How can you give out of a pure heart, with no hidden motive, knowing that God will reward you?
>
> 2. What reward, or recognition, system can you set up for your people to help them become more giving at work, in their projects, without doing their work for recognition?

97

GIVING IN SECRET

MATTHEW 6:3-4

With some of His audience nodding their heads in agreement, Jesus could see He was getting through, even though He was talking about some pretty heavy concepts. As He told them that God has rewards for them, He also told them to do their giving in secret.

> **LEADERSHIP TIP #78**
>
> Give the gifts God directs you to give in the privacy of your own heart and mind, as well as in a private place.

Now, the word Jesus used for "secret," actually means a "hiding place." The idea is that no one else should know what the giving person is doing.

Why can't other people know I'm giving? His listeners must have been thinking. As long as they were doing it out of pure motives, what difference would it make if anyone else knew about it?

Apparently, giving in secret was a motive-check that Jesus gave His followers. He wanted them to make sure they really were giving for the right reason.

1. What does it mean to give your gifts in the "privacy of your own heart and mind?"

2. How is Jesus' teaching about giving in secret compatible with letting everyone see your good deeds (Matthew 5:16)?

Individual Prayer

MATTHEW 6:5-6

After Jesus taught His followers to give in secret, out of pure motives, He also told them where to pray. His instruction for praying was in line with His teaching on giving. Do it privately. "When you pray," He said, "go into your room, close the door and pray to your Father, who is unseen."

> **LEADERSHIP TIP #79**
>
> Pray in the privacy of your own heart rather than to be praised by others for your fine words.

Now, doesn't that fly in the face of people praying openly as a group? No, not really. Jesus was speaking about an individual talking with God. Not a group of people talking with Him.

Here's His point. Religious leaders in Jesus' day would often individually pray out loud in public. Their motive was to be praised for their deep "spirituality." Jesus was against that way of praying because of their impure motives. He taught that prayer should be a sincere and pure connection with God. That would be tough to have where lots of people are milling around. When praying out loud in public, it would be difficult not to be aware that other people were looking. And, knowing other people were looking could be a distraction.

1. How does giving to others relate to your private praying to God?

2. What do you need to be praying for those you are leading?

Sincerity in Prayer

MATTHEW 6:7

"When you pray," Jesus said, as He continued teaching the crowd about praying, "don't talk on and on as people do who don't know God." Jesus had a deep understanding of the religious practices of His day, especially as the high and mighty Pharisees modeled them. The Pharisees didn't talk to God the same way they talked to each other.

LEADERSHIP TIP #80

When you talk to God, say what's on your mind, but don't keep going on and on with the same words.

When they prayed, they often took on a "holy" tone, and talked on and on. Then, they would repeat the same sentences over and over, and in a variety of ways. Their "babbling" implied the "religious showoffs" weren't really tuned into God when they were praying. It was as if they were trying to wear God down. Instead, other people got tired just listening. Yet, the Pharisees were the only model for praying the people had. That is, until Jesus came along. The point of Jesus' instruction? He wanted His followers to be just as real in their talking to God as they were in talking to each other.

1. How is talking to God similar to talking to other people, and in what way is it different?

2. How might "babbling" and the frequent repetition of words indicate the person is not really tuned in to God?

God Already Knows

MATTHEW 6:8

As Jesus talked about prayer, His listeners were paying close attention. Especially His newly selected team of twelve. They had already seen the results of their leader's prayer. They had seen the power, day after day. So, Jesus' next insight about prayer might have puzzled His twelve a bit.

> **LEADERSHIP TIP #81**
>
> Just as God knows your needs, work at knowing the needs of the people you lead.

He said, "Your Father knows what you need before you ask Him."

So, the obvious question going through His listener's minds, why pray? Wouldn't God's knowing what His people needed, before they prayed, be the same as they knowing what someone else needed, before they asked for help? If they did what Jesus taught them to do, and helped the person without being asked, why wouldn't God do the same without being asked?

1. If God knows what you need before you present your needs to Him, why doesn't He supply your needs without you having to go to Him in prayer?

2. What might God knowing your needs say to you about you knowing the needs of the people you lead?

3. God knows your needs without your telling Him because He is God. So, how can you get to know the needs of the people you lead?

The Model Prayer
God as Father

MATTHEW 6:9

Once Jesus tweaked the curiosity of His audience, He taught them a model for praying that would get results. His idea was that prayer moves God to do what He wants to do, but won't do, without His people praying. Prayer is a tool of connection. That's why, even though God knows what Jesus' followers need before they ask, they still need to ask to get His help.

> **LEADERSHIP TIP #82**
>
> Approach God in prayer as your "daddy." He loves you with every fiber of who He is.

Jesus started out by teaching His people to call God, "Father." Whatever mental picture His listeners had of "father," it didn't measure up to what Jesus had in mind. His Father was consistently loving, sacrificing, giving, caring, compassionate, helpful, and a host of other positive adjectives. Jesus described God as a "daddy" who was genuinely interested in His people beyond anything they could ever imagine. And, in spite of who they were, He loved them. As a "daddy."

1. What does it mean that prayer is a tool of connection?

2. Why does Jesus want you to start all of your talking to God seeing Him as your Father?

THE MODEL PRAYER
PRAISING GOD

MATTHEW 6:9

After Jesus' listeners got into their minds that God was their Father, He taught them to spend some time praising God. His idea of praising God, in the words, "hallowed be Your name," meant recognizing God for His greatness. Not just for what He could do for a person, but for who He

LEADERSHIP TIP #83

Spend the first part of your time with God in prayer, praising Him for who He is.

is. Among other things Jesus had in mind, God is all-knowing, He's present everywhere at the same time, and He has the absolute and total power to do anything He wishes to do. That means He can grant a request, or deny it.

God created every one of the billions and billions of stars in each galaxy, and He has a name for each of them (Psalm 147:4). He even knows the exact number of hairs on each person's head, regardless of how many or few the person has (Luke 12:7). That's what Jesus wanted His followers to be thinking about as they approached their Father. Who He really is.

1. Why does Jesus think it's important to praise God before making any request of Him? Is that the same as "buttering" Him up?

2. How can the book of Psalms help you praise God?

THE MODEL PRAYER
THE KINGDOM

MATTHEW 6:10

Next, Jesus said to pray for the "Kingdom of God" to come. Now, the "Kingdom of God" is anyplace where God is the absolute ruler. Anyplace where He is the king.

The purpose of Jesus on earth was to build that Kingdom. His strategy was simple and direct. He would first build the

> **LEADERSHIP TIP #84**
>
> Ask God to bring His Kingdom to each of the people you lead, and to all those they influence through your product or service.

Kingdom in the hearts of people. Then, when the time on earth for recruiting people into that Kingdom of hearts had come to an end, Jesus would set up the physical Kingdom on a new earth (Revelation 21:1-4). The new earth would take the place of the existing planet.

It would be physical place where all His people would live together in companionship, adventure, and total peace. A place where God would lovingly rule. And, a place Jesus' followers would enjoy being together in a forever family. Jesus taught His followers to ask God to bring the spiritual Kingdom into the hearts of people, and to usher in the physical Kingdom on the new earth.

> What are specific ways you can use your product or service more directly in building God's kingdom?

THE MODEL PRAYER
GOD'S WILL

MATTHEW 6:10

Jesus then added another detail to what it meant to ask for God's Kingdom to come. He taught His followers, in addition, to ask for God's will to be done on earth, just as He does it in Heaven itself. So, why was this a request Jesus taught the people sitting on the slope in front of Him?

> **LEADERSHIP TIP #85**
>
> Ask God what His will for you is each day. Then, with Jesus living in and through you, do it. Also, ask God to show His will to specific people He puts on your mind.

It might have been for followers of Jesus to take their responsibility seriously. You see, He gave His people the assignment of learning from God what His will was for them each moment of the day. Then, once they did know His plan, through His strength, they were to do it. It wasn't a matter of just knowing, but also doing.

Jesus also wanted His people to be praying this same request for other people in their lives. Why? So each of those people might line up with God's plan for their lives, as well.

---

1. How is doing God's will somewhat different than having His kingdom in your heart, or, is it?

2. What steps will you take to develop rules for your work, and the people you lead, that are based on God's will?

THE MODEL PRAYER
DAILY BREAD

MATTHEW 6:11

Jesus knew that, sometimes, His audience confused their "wants" with their "needs." He also understood that, compared to their wants, they really needed only a few things, such as shelter, food, water, and clothing, When Jesus taught His people to ask God for

LEADERSHIP TIP #86

Each day, ask God to supply your specific needs.

"daily bread," He was focusing on their needs. Your see, the word "bread" Jesus used referred to any need a person had. Not just the food he ate.

Also, Jesus was teaching His disciples to ask God for "bread" each day, not weekly. So, why daily, and no longer than just 24 hours at a time? Well, Jesus knew how easy it was for people to start taking God for granted. That's why God supplied the Jews in the wilderness enough manna for only one day at a time. It helped His people know they could trust Him.

Jesus implied that God would supply daily needs as His people asked Him. The key, Jesus taught, was to make the request, and God would do it. How God would do it was up to Him.

What experience have you had in God supplying your needs only one day at a time?

The Model Prayer

FORGIVENESS

Matthew 6:12

Jesus then helped His disciples realize a difference between having a relationship with God, and having close fellowship with Him. He tied the fellowship they had with each other to the fellowship they had with God.

> **LEADERSHIP TIP #87**
>
> To experience a closer fellowship with God, ask Him to help you forgive anyone who has wronged you.

For example, if James did wrong to John, the two brothers would feel at odds with each other. Their fellowship would be strained. Yet, they would still be in a family relationship. The same was true with their tie-in to God. James and John were in God's family. Yet, at the same time they were in His family, they could also be out of fellowship with Him.

Jesus wanted all of His followers to understand this key issue. When God's people are out of fellowship with someone who has wronged them, they are also out of fellowship with God. Why? Because God uses followers of Jesus to model His ways to the world. When His followers are out of fellowship with others, they're also out of step with God's plan for them. As a result, their fellowship with God is strained.

> How can you help the people you lead forgive each other of the wrongs they have experienced?

The Model Prayer
RESISTING TEMPTATION

Matthew 6:13

Jesus knew, from first-hand experience, temptation was always lurking in the shadows. It was for Him, and it would be for His followers, too. Satan would make sure of that. Therefore, Jesus taught His disciples to pray, "Lead us not into temptation."

> **LEADERSHIP TIP #88**
>
> Ask God to lead you away from any temptation that would get you out of step with Him.

Now, was Jesus implying God would be tempting His followers to do wrong if they didn't ask Him not to tempt them? No. You see, the term, "lead us not into temptation," is a permissive imperative. Jesus was actually teaching His followers to pray, "Lead us away from temptation."

That's why He then added to the request, "Deliver us from the evil one." Jesus knew that Satan and his army were always trying to get His own followers off course. Just like Satan personally had tried to do with Jesus in the wilderness.

1. In the Bible, the word temptation can mean a "testing," or it can mean a solicitation for doing wrong. How do we know temptation, in this teaching, refers to a solicitation for doing wrong?

2. What can you do to eliminate as much temptation as possible from your own life, as well as from the people you lead?

Fasting for Closeness

Matthew 6:16-18

Immediately, after giving His followers a model for praying to get God's results, Jesus taught them about fasting. Now, He Himself fasted in the wilderness. Not just because there wasn't much food in that parched area, but because it was also a discipline that helped Him be close to His Father.

LEADERSHIP TIP #89

Fast to draw close to God, especially before making big decisions.

Healthwise, the fast does have a purifying affect on the physical body. Going without food for an extended period helps flush out toxins. However, as it purifies the body, fasting also has a purifying influence on one's mind. And, one's connection to God. Jesus knew that fasting could help a person be more sensitive to God, and to what God wanted him to do.

On the other hand, religious leaders in Jesus' day used fasting to draw attention to how spiritual they were. Or, appeared to be. They didn't fast, necessarily, as a means to draw closer to God. So, in this teaching, Jesus was warning His followers against fasting to draw attention to themselves. Yes, they should fast. But, as a discipline to draw closer to God.

How might fasting help you get God's leading for taking your work to the next level, and what will you do about it?

Storing Up Treasures

MATTHEW 6:19-21

Jesus knew, in a materialistic world, that what He was about to say would not be accepted...at first, that is. When He told the attentive crowd, sitting in front of Him, not to store up treasures on earth, He was not saying material things were bad. In fact, He had just told the people to ask God for their daily bread, or the supplies for their daily needs.

LEADERSHIP TIP #90

See your work, and all of your material possessions, as vehicles for building God's Kingdom.

So, what was He saying? Jesus was teaching not to store up material things as if they'll last forever. Again, He's right in line with what He had just taught about the "daily" part of asking for "daily bread."

Here's what He was saying. As His followers would strive to build God's Kingdom in the hearts of people, God would take care of their material needs. They wouldn't have to store them up. Jesus knew that whatever His disciples treasured would capture their hearts and minds. He wanted that to be God's New World, and nothing else.

1. How can you be even more focused in using your work, and material possessions, to help build God's Kingdom?

2. How can you help your people develop an eternal perspective?

110

EVALUATING PRIORITIES

MATTHEW 6:19-21

That day, on the grassy slope, Jesus told the huge crowd, "Wherever your treasure is, there the desires of your heart will also be." When He said that, He might have been wanting them to do a quick "priority-check."

LEADERSHIP TIP #91

Evaluate your priorities by observing where your thoughts and energies are directed most of the time.

Since their hearts and thoughts were with their treasure, what were they thinking about the most? Was it what they were going to eat for the next meal? Perhaps it was how to work the next deal coming up. Maybe some in Jesus' inner group might have had financial concerns. How were they going to get out of debt, since they had just started following Him full time? Or, how could they still make a living?

Jesus knew His people first had to determine what they were thinking about the most. That would tip them off as to what they treasured the most. Then, once they knew what they treasured the most, they could evaluate if that treasure should really be their top priority.

1. What steps will you take to make your top priorities thinking and doing those things that have an eternal consequence?

2. How can you help your people take a "priority-check?"

THE EYE AS A LAMP

MATTHEW 6:22-23

The open windows of a Palestinian house let sunlight shine in the house to light it up. Of course, when the sun went down, and it got dark inside, the people would have to light their oil lamps to light up the house.

LEADERSHIP TIP #92

Allow only what is valued by God to come into your mind and body through your eyes.

Jesus likened their body to a house, with their eyes being a lamp sitting on a stand inside the house. He said, "Your eye is a lamp that provides light for your body. When your eye is good, your whole body is filled with light. But when your eye is bad, your whole body is filled with darkness." Interestingly, Jesus used the word for body that included the mind.

What was Jesus' point? He knew one's mind could cause the "darkness" of disease in the body. Just as it could cause the "light" of health. So, whatever His followers allowed to come into their minds, through their eyes, it could affect the health of their physical body, as well as their entire life.

1. How can what you watch on TV actually be a factor in either causing health or disease in your body?

2. What can you do to help the people you lead use their eyes to improve their physical health, as well as their entire life?

SERVING TWO MASTERS

MATTHEW 6:24

Jesus was a keen student of people. He knew a person's mind could focus only on one thing, at a 100% capacity, at a time. A divided mind would lead to a less effective lifestyle.

LEADERSHIP TIP #93

Make an all-out commitment to serve God with your total heart, rather than to keep looking for material wealth and comfort.

That's why He warned His listeners: "No one can serve two masters. For you will hate one and love the other; you will be devoted to one and despise the other. You cannot serve both God and money." In this teaching, Jesus was warning His followers about having a lifestyle with one foot in God's Kingdom and the other in the world.

Now, the word Jesus used for "master" implies one who has absolute ownership. And, the word He used for "serve" means to serve as a slave. The idea He wanted to get across is that it was not possible to be a slave to two "absolute owners." His followers would either love one and hate the other, or it would be the other way around. They can't serve two opposing masters at 100% of their capacity. It just can't be done. Jesus challenged His followers to make their choice.

How can you help those you lead sharpen their focus on God and what He has in store for them?

113

Worries of Life

MATTHEW 6:25-32

Pagans in Jesus' time did not believe in God. As a result, they constantly worried about the needs of life. Jesus saw that "worry" all around Him as He walked the roads, mixing with people.

LEADERSHIP TIP #94

By keeping in mind God knows exactly what you need, you won't be anxious about the necessities of life.

One of the traits that would set His followers aside from all other people would be a total tranquility about those same necessities. "Can all your worries," He asked, wanting them to get perspective, "add a single moment to your life?"

Of course, He knew it would be just the opposite. Worry and stress tend to shorten one's life. He could see, throughout the land, how anxiety actually caused terrible diseases.

Jesus wanted His followers to know that God was aware of all their needs. His message? Trust God -- totally -- and He would remove their worry. Absolute and unswerving trust in God. That's what Jesus wanted all of His followers to demonstrate to the worry-filled world around them. The kind of trust in God that Jesus Himself modeled to each of them.

What steps will you take to leave each of your worries in the capable hands of God, and to train your people to do the same?

114

THE MAIN PURSUIT

MATTHEW 6:33

In His next instruction, Jesus gave the crowd a "formula" for living a worry-free life. "Seek the Kingdom of God above all else, and live God's way," He said, "and He will give you everything you need."

Jesus was actually promising that God would take care of all of their needs.

> ## LEADERSHIP TIP #95
>
> Direct all of your time and energy toward doing things God's way in everything He calls you to do, and He will take care of what you need.

Now, wait a minute, some of His listeners must have been thinking. *That doesn't sound right. Is Jesus saying all we have to do is sit back and watch God take care of us? Is He saying we don't have to lift a finger to supply our own needs?*

No to both questions. Here's what Jesus was saying. First, He wanted His followers to apply God's values and His ways to their work, and to their life. Second, He wanted His followers to be caught up in recruiting others to God's Kingdom, as well as in teaching them God's ways. Third, as His followers did those two things, God would supply them with what they needed from day to day. That was His amazing promise.

1. Why did Jesus make such a fantastic promise?

2. What do you have to change to put all of your energy into first seeking God's Kingdom in your life?

Living in the Present Tense

"So don't worry about tomorrow," Jesus said, in continuing His thought, "for tomorrow will bring its own worries. Today's trouble is enough for today." Jesus taught His followers to live in the present tense. Yet, He also taught them to look forward to their eternal homeland. So, how could they keep looking toward their future, and still live at 100% in the present?

LEADERSHIP TIP #96

Develop the same focus on the future eternal Kingdom that Jesus had, and you will have more passion for the present.

Peter, Andrew, James, John and the rest of them only had to look at Jesus Himself. He was their example for how to merge two seemingly contrary approaches to life. Jesus had the future Kingdom engraved in His mind. He knew it well. That's why He so energetically recruited people to go there. His passion for the future gave Him His passion for the present.

That's the same merged approach Jesus taught His followers to have. To etch the future Kingom in their mind, and to totally rely on God for the present. That was His key to a worry-free life. The present and future were both in God's hands.

How will you give your people a future orientation in their work that will give them even more passion for the now?

CRITICIZING OTHERS

MATTHEW 7:1-2

Life in God's Kingdom will be totally free of one person criticizing another. So, to bring that quality home to the crowd, Jesus said, "Don't judge others, and you won't be judged. For you will be treated as you treat others. Yes, the standard you use in judging is the same standard by which you will be judged." Now, in the context Jesus was teaching, He implied "judging" was making a quick, and unfair, criticism.

LEADERSHIP TIP #97

Don't judgmentally censor, or criticize, the actions of others unless you want the same unfair treatment given you.

So, why shouldn't His followers make judgments like that? Well, first, a person judging like that wouldn't have all the facts. Without knowing those facts, he could neither be fair, nor accurate. Second, and this is the main point of Jesus' teaching. The person judging, in turn, would be judged with the same unfair measurement he had used. Unfairly judging others only invites the same unfair treatment. Jesus didn't want His followers to be caught up in making petty criticisms of others.

1. What are some of the problems that unfairly judging others can cause?

2. How can you keep from unfairly criticizing someone else?

The Teacher and Student

LUKE 6:39-40

"Can one blind person lead another?" Jesus asked the people, perhaps gazing directly at His own men. "Won't they both fall into a ditch? Students are not greater than their teacher. But the student who is fully trained will become like the teacher." Jesus' idea was that a student, or "blind" person, should follow somone who knew where they were going. Not another person who really was no more than a student himself.

> **LEADERSHIP TIP #98**
>
> To multiply yourself, train others to do what you do, and how you do it.

Now, what was the advantage of a student following a "sighted," or, real, teacher? With hard work, that student will someday become like his teacher. What a great compliment. To have students who apply what the teacher teaches, and, in the long run, become like him. Jesus understood a teacher was a leader, and a leader must be a teacher. Great leaders are not just fantastic vision-givers and motivators. They're also great teachers. They know how to put ideas into the minds of people, and present ways to do things better. When a teacher sees his students becoming like him, he knows he has done his job. Jesus wanted His followers to become like Him.

> What principles do you want to teach your people, and what steps will you take to teach those principles?

A SPECK OF DUST AND A LOG

PART ONE

MATTHEW 7:3-5

In Jesus' typically good sense of humor, He then contrasted two pieces of wood. Perhaps with comical hand gestures, He described one as a huge log, and the other as a miniscule piece of sawdust. Ironically, He said the huge log was in the eye of one person, and the little speck was in the

> ## LEADERSHIP TIP #99
>
> Be sure you're not guilty of a similar kind of wrong doing before you try to help someone else with theirs.

eye of a second person. Jesus likened a person who was quick to judge, or criticize, another as having the huge log in his eye. Yet, in spite of the log, that person actually thought he could see clearly to remove the tiny speck of sawdust from the other person's eye.

Jesus "saw" it differently. "Hypocrite!" He said, "First get rid of the log in your own eye; then you will see well enough to deal with the speck in your friend's eye." Jesus' idea was, everyone has faults. He wanted His followers, who had faults, to first take care of their own problems. Then, the other person would be more open to their valid criticism, and their much needed help.

> You'll always have some sort of problems. So, how can you ever try to help someone else deal with theirs?

119

A Speck of Dust and a Log

Part Two

Matthew 7:3-5

Now, let's put a slightly different twist on this same teaching of Jesus. Sometimes, even before His followers take care of the log in their own eye, they allow criticism of someone to roll out of their mouth. It shouldn't, but it does.

> **LEADERSHIP TIP #100**
>
> Use your initial criticism of someone else to correct a similar type of weakness in yourself.

So, how can they turn that negative into something positive? Well, they can't keep their "escaped" criticism from stinging the other person. So, there still is a negative to it. However, they can use their criticism to remind them of the log remaining in their own eye. Then, they can do something about it. Once they own up to their own shortcomings, they can try to help the other person they hurt with their criticism.

1. Is it ever all right to help someone get rid of the "speck" in their eye, when you still have a "log" in your own eye? And, if so, under what conditions?

2. How can you deal with weaknesses in your life without becoming overly introspective?

3. How can you help the people you lead deal with weaknesses in their lives when you aren't perfect?

Pearls Before Swine

Matthew 7:6

Jesus knew that communication would always be a challenge for His team. Whether they were passing on one of His teachings to an unbelieving townsperson, or telling someone how God answered one of their own prayer requests.

> ## LEADERSHIP TIP #101
>
> Be discerning with whom you share spiritual truths, since a spiritually insensitive person will attack the truths, instead of listen to them.

So, perhaps with a tossing motion, He said, "Don't throw your pearls to pigs. If you do, they may trample them under their feet. Then they'll turn and tear you to pieces."

The people had seen many pig pens in the Gentile areas they had visited. They knew that, if they tossed a few pearls into a pig pen, they probably would never see those pearls again. A pig just can't appreciate a pearl, no matter how valuable it is. In fact, a pig might even attack a person who was scrounging around in its pen, looking for the pearls. In this teaching, Jesus was simply telling His followers to use good judgment in passing on spiritual truths. If a person was angry with God for some reason, that person could direct his anger with God against the person sharing. His point? Share at the right time.

1. How will you know what spiritual truth to share with a person?

2. How might this same teaching apply to training your people with what they need to know to be more effective?

RELENTLESS PRAYER

MATTHEW 7:7-11

Jesus, then, turned His attention to His most useful "tool" in staying connected to His Father, prayer. "Ask and it will be given to you," He said, "seek and you will find; knock and the door will be opened to you."

Then He explained why people should be relentless in prayer requests. "For everyone who asks

> **LEADERSHIP TIP #102**
>
> Keep on bringing your same requests to God in prayer, keep on looking for His answers, and keep on testing each possible answer to see if it is from God.

receives; he who seeks finds; and to him who knocks, the door will be opened." Now, the verbs "ask," "seek," and "knock" are all in the present tense. That means each action is ongoing, and it's overlapping with the other actions. Once the process is started, all the actions continue on at the same time.

Why should people be so relentless in bringing their requests to God? One reason. One reason only. So they could truly experience God. So they could experience Him through real, answered prayer requests. Just like Jesus did.

> 1. How will you know if an opportunity that presents Itself, as you continue in prayer, is God's answer?
>
> 2. What if God didn't act unless you prayed for someone, or something?

THE GOLDEN RULE

MATTHEW 7:12

Jesus now gave His people a lesson that has been passed down through the centuries. No matter what relationship a person has with God. It's popularly called The Golden Rule: "Do unto others what you would have them do unto you." It's also referred to as the Mount Everest of Ethics.

> **LEADERSHIP TIP #103**
>
> Make treating others the same way you want to be treated the foundation of your relating to others.

The idea is we all want to be treated right. That's part of our natural make-up. So, in order to motivate people to treat them right, Jesus taught His followers, treat others right. Look out for the good of others, not just for their own good.

Like in all of Jesus' teachings, He Himself was the perfect model of what He was saying. What a great practice for follower-leaders in all walks of life. In fact, this teaching should also be called the Mount Everest of Leadership.

1. What are three ways you want other people to treat you?

2. What will you do to consistently treat other people in those same three ways?

3. How can you implement The Golden Rule in your work, and communicate it to the people you serve?

WIDE AND NARROW GATES

MATTHEW 7:13-14

Jesus possibly shook His head slightly. Then, He looked directly at the men and women sitting closest to Him. He made it clear. Yes, He was fully convinced.

LEADERSHIP TIP #104

Concentrate only on God's "narrow road" way of doing your work, even though many attractive alternatives from the world are available.

"You can enter God's Kingdom only through the narrow gate. The highway to hell is broad, and its gate is wide for the many who choose that way. But the gateway to life is very narrow, and the road is difficult." Then, perhaps with a sadness in His eyes, He said, "Only a few ever find it."

Jesus knew some of those people in front of Him were on the broad highway. Even worse, many of them didn't even know it. Later, Jesus would tell His followers that the narrow road heading to Heaven went through Him (John 14:6). Good works would never be the issue. Needless to say, Jesus' slant was pretty narrow-minded. But, truth is narrow-minded. Two plus two will always equal four. That fact is narrow-minded.

Nevertheless, it is true.

1. What steps will you take to build the principles of your business, team, or organization, on God's "narrow road" approach?
2. How will you train your people on doing things God's way?

EVERY FOLLOWER A LEADER & EVERY LEADER A FOLLOWER

THE FRUIT OF A PERSON

MATTHEW 7:15-20

Jesus quickly swung the thoughts of His listeners, from people walking on two different roads, to how to read the people on those roads. The context of what He taught was knowing whether a prophet was the real thing, or not. However, what He said would apply to "reading" anyone.

LEADERSHIP TIP #105

Evaluate each person you lead by the results of his actions over time, rather than by his outward appearance.

Perhaps He pointed to a tree on the hillside, loaded with wild fruit, as He put in plain words how to do it. "Just as you can identify a tree by its fruit," He explained, "so you can identify people by their actions."

Jesus was saying a healthy apple is the result of a healthy tree. A healthy grape is the result of a healthy vine. So, once again, Jesus used the example of nature to reveal a truth. This time, in assessing who people really are. He was saying that, over time, look at the actions of a person. That's how one can know who people really are. Beyond their appearance.

1. In what ways have specific people done, or not done, what you've asked of them, and what does that tell you about them?

2. What program, or method, can you install that will help you evaluate the production of your people?

125

Words Versus Actions

MATTHEW 7:21

Jesus knew what was inside the hearts of people. He knew that some people always said the right things. They simply knew the lingo. In fact, some of those sitting on the ground in front of Him might have been like that. But, when you looked closely at them, their actions didn't back up their words.

> **LEADERSHIP TIP #106**
>
> Look first for supporting actions to back up a person's words. Then you will get a leaning as to what a person really believes.

Jesus, most likely, baffled His listeners when He declared, "Not everyone who says to me, 'Lord, Lord,' will enter the Kingdom of Heaven. Only those who actually do the will of my Father in Heaven will enter." Jesus taught His followers to first look at a person's immediate actions. Is the person caught up in doing the will of God? As Jesus' next teaching will indicate, this isn't the only way to tell what's really in a person's heart. Sometimes a person can masquerade and cover things up for a bit. But, it is a start. Do the actions support the words?

1. What actions will you look for in your people to see what their relationship with God is?

2. How can you help a person who says one thing, but whose actions don't back up his words?

False Spiritual Leaders

Matthew 7:22-23

Jesus continued His teaching on "reading" people. This time, with a warning. He could see in people the built-in emptiness in their heart that only God could fill. He knew it was a longing everyone had, even though it could go unrecognized for a time in a person's life.

LEADERSHIP TIP #107

Don't be taken in by a person simply because he outwardly does what is considered to be spiritual activities. Look for what is really in the person's heart.

Then, of course, there was the religious establishment. Men who, for the most part, paraded around looking pious, but who were mainly just absorbed in themselves.

Jesus saw it the very first time He and His family celebrated the Passover together in Jerusalem. Even as a young boy, Jesus saw imposters who were never authorized by God to be His spokespeople. He didn't even consider them to be in God's Kingdom. They were full of self-importance. They had never come to God on His terms, empty of themselves. He warned that, on judgment day, He will tell them, "I never knew you. Get away from me, you who break God's laws."

1. How can you tell false spiritual teachers from the real thing?

2. What might this teaching say to you personally about leading others?

A HOUSE BUILT ON ROCK

MATTHEW 7:24-25

Jesus had been teaching the sun-drenched crowd, including His own disciples, for quite some time. Now, He wanted to wrap it all up with a word picture that would stick in their minds. Especially every time a violent, torrent of rain hit the land.

> **LEADERSHIP TIP #108**
>
> Take time each day to listen to Jesus through His teachings. Then, commit yourself to put into practice what you hear from Him in your life, including your place of work.

Reaching into His own bag of experiences as a carpenter, Jesus knew the value of building a house on a foundation of solid rock. Even as a boy growing up, He probably had heard of houses collapsing in storms and the floods caused by those storms. Houses that were foolishly built on the soft, and shifting ground. Not on a good foundation.

He said, "Anyone who listens to my teaching and follows it is wise, like a person who builds a house on solid rock." Jesus called the people to do two things. First, listen to Him. So far, so good. That's what they had been doing. Second, obey His words. Jesus equated a person who did those two things, listen and obey, to a house that was built on solid rock. That person could endure the torrent of tough situations in life.

> In what way might you need to shore up the foundation upon which you live, and lead?

A House Built on Sand

MATTHEW 7:26-27

Jesus used the same verb for "hear," or "listen" in His first teaching about building a house on solid rock, as He did in His second teaching. The one about building a house on sandy ground.

> **LEADERSHIP TIP #109**
>
> Make sure the people you lead know Jesus' warning about the "house on sand" person. Both their present and future life depend on it.

He said, "Anyone who hears my teaching and doesn't obey it is foolish, like a person who builds a house on sand." In each teaching, Jesus described a person who actually did listen to Him. Both "listeners" had the truth. That was good. However, that's where the similarity ended. The "house on solid rock" listener obeyed the truth of what Jesus taught; the "house on sand" listener ignored it.

Jesus called such a person "foolish." That's a strong word describing a dull and slow person. Then, Jesus explained what would happen to such a foolish person. That person would cave-in, and fall to pieces in the storms of life. Just like a house built on sand. As Jesus ended His lessons for the day, He gave fair warning to everyone. The "house on sand" person's lack of action would cause his own collapse. There would be no one else to blame.

> What steps will you take to bring this warning of Jesus to the people in your world of influence?

129

A ROMAN OFFICER'S FAITH

LUKE 7:1-10

After Jesus and His men walked down from the mountain, they went back to Capernaum, Peter's hometown. It was their new headquarters by the lake. Now, as they were entering the area, a Roman officer's slave was dying. The officer, hearing that Jesus was back in town, quickly sent

> **LEADERSHIP TIP #110**
>
> Demonstrate your reliance on Jesus in practical ways each day at work, and you'll be pleasing to Him.

some Jewish leaders to ask Jesus to heal his dying slave. Apparently, the Roman officer had done many acts of kindness for the Jews. That was unusual for any Roman to do.

Jesus hurried with His guides along the narrow street leading to the officer's house. However, before He could enter, which would have been degrading for a Jew to enter an "unclean" Gentile's house, the officer rushed out of the door. He didn't want Jesus to shame Himself. He said, "Just say the word and my servant will be healed." Jesus was amazed and impressed by the strong faith of a Gentile. That was the "total reliance" kind of faith He had been calling His own people, the Jews, to experience. He saw it first in a Gentile.

1. How do obedience and faith relate to each other?

2. In leading your people, in what specific ways can you demonstrate more of a reliance on Jesus?

130

RAISING A DEAD BOY

LUKE 7:11-17

Jesus and His men went back on the road. As they were walking through the gateway of the village of Nain, they saw a funeral procession coming their way. Now, at a village's gateway, or entrance, people would gather to catch up on the latest news.

> **LEADERHIP TIP #111**
>
> In tangible ways, show compassion to those you lead who are hurting, and teach your people to do the same.

So, no doubt, Jesus had been hearing people talk about the huge loss for their neighbor, a widow lady. Her only son had died. Typically, in those days, widows were penniless. Women didn't work outside of the house. Consequently, without her son, this woman had no way to bring in money. No way, without begging, or receiving help from her friends, that is.

With His Father's deep compassion stirring inside of Him, Jesus walked up to the procession, put His hand on the coffin, and stopped it. That was a religious no-no. And, Jesus knew it. Anyone touching a coffin carrying a body was thought of as "unclean." But, with no regard for taboos, Jesus spoke the words, "Young man, get up!" Amazingly, the boy did.

> What steps will you take to be sure you know about the heartaches of those you are leading?

AN OUTCAST WOMAN
PART ONE

LUKE 7:36-50

As news spread about what Jesus did in Nain, He accepted a banquet invitation from a Pharisee named Simon. Jesus was stretching out on a bench alongside of the banquet table, when a woman, known for her immorality, quietly walked over from the onlooker section. She knelt down at

LEADERSHIP TIP #112

Keep in mind how much God has forgiven you, and your love for Him will grow.

Jesus' feet, and started sobbing. In fact, so many tears were flowing, they were dropping on His feet. The woman dried His feet with her long flowing hair. Then she rubbed an expensive perfume on them. People wondered what was happening.

The host was thinking, *If Jesus were from God, He wouldn't allow such a sinner to do that.* However, Jesus quickly, read Simon's thoughts. He told the host a story about two people who had been forgiven different sums of money. Then He asked, "Who loved the most?" Simon answered, "The one who was forgiven the most." "Right you are," Jesus replied, perhaps with a penetrating look. Then, after scolding Simon for not showing the normal courtesies to his guests, Jesus turned to the woman and said, "Your sins are forgiven."

How might this application also work between you and the people you lead?

132

AN OUTCAST WOMAN

PART TWO

LUKE 7:36-50

The perfume the outcast woman rubbed on Jesus' feet was not the ordinary "brand." It was not the kind she could have bought at the local "supermarket." It was the most expensive perfume in a very limited market.

> **LEADERSHIP TIP #113**
>
> Express your love for Jesus by giving Him the best quality of everything you have and do.

Just a tiny amount would have cost her a small fortune. She would have used this kind of perfume only on very special occasions. So, why did the woman, who probably wasn't wealthy, use her best, and most treasured perfume, on Jesus' feet? It wasn't as if the people at the banquet could smell the perfume. They couldn't appreciate its worth.

However, Jesus could, and He did. He recognized the value of what she was doing. As Jesus watched her, He knew it was because the woman was so grateful. Grateful for all that God had forgiven her through Him, even before He confirmed it to her. He knew the woman wanted her gift to represent the quality of her love for Him. That's why Jesus allowed her to do it. It was her expression of love. No lesser perfume would do.

> What areas of your work do you need to upgrade if what you do is to match your love for Jesus?

JESUS' TRUE FAMILY

MATTHEW 12:46-50

On another day, Jesus was inside a house teaching people about the Kingdom of God. Someone called to Him through the open doorway, "Your mother and brothers are outside, and they want to talk to you."

LEADERSHIP TIP #114

See other followers of Jesus, regardless of their backgrounds, as your true and forever family.

Everyone in the house was surprised when, instead of immediately going out to see his family, Jesus asked a rhetorical question. "Who is my mother, and who are my brothers?" Then, most likely surprising His disciples, and causing them to raise their eyebrows, Jesus pointed at them and said, "These are my mother and brothers. Whoever does the will of my Father in heaven is my brother and sister and mother."

Now, why did Jesus say that? Didn't He want to visit with his blood family? Sure He did, and we can be sure that Jesus did visit with them. Yet, He said what He did to get across a great truth about real family. Real family is more a matter of spirit than it is of blood.

1. Who are your true family in your work?

2. What can you do to help develop family togetherness with your family at work?

Parables by the Lakeside

MATTHEW 13:1-52

Jesus loved spending time at the lake. In fact, He seemed to enjoy everything about the open air. He also had a keen eye for the life what was going on around Him. He didn't miss a thing.

LEADERSHIP TIP #115

Use graphic stories people can understand to effectively communicate your feelings, ideas, and values.

Because of His passion for the outdoors, He told many stories about life outside, stories that communicated God's principles. Among other things, He talked about farmers and the planting of crops, as well as birds and how they lived.

One day when His followers asked why He used stories time and time again in His teachings, He answered, "Because people see what I do, but they don't really see. They hear what I say, but they don't really hear, and they don't understand."

After that Jesus explained it to those gathered around Him. A person who really wanted to get a grip on God's truths would understand His stories. Yes, He told stories to communicate truths. However, Jesus also told stories to make a sharp division between people who loved God, and those who didn't.

What is the best story you can tell to your people to communicate what you want them to accomplish?

Calming a Storm

Part One

MARK 4:35-41

Jesus spent most of the day teaching crowds by the lake. Then, as tired as He was, He climbed into one of His friend's boats and said, "Let's go over to the other side of the lake." His friends quickly got into the boat, and they set sail. Well, no sooner had Jesus stretched out on a cushion in the back, He slipped off into a deep sleep.

> **LEADERSHIP TIP #116**
>
> Excel as a student of Jesus, and keep asking, "Who is this man?" as you read about Him in the Bible.

All was smooth, until a strong wind suddenly swept down from snow-capped, Mount Hermon in the north. It churned up the lake. And, in no time, a violent storm was raging, tossing the boat, with a bunch of frightened men and a sleeping leader, from one wave to another.

After one of His men frantically woke Him up, Jesus managed to pull Himself to His feet. Then, holding on to a staff, He shouted, "Peace, be still." His men were amazed. The wind abruptly stopped. The waves collapsed into a smooth, glassy lake. With his eyes wide open in surprise, a drenched disciple asked, "Who is this man?"

What does it mean to excel as a student of Jesus, and how would that role impact how you lead?

Calming a Storm

Part Two

Mark 4:35-41

Let's take a moment to focus on what Jesus asked His men right after He calmed the storm. "Why are you so afraid?" He asked. "Do you still not have faith in me?" It was a legitimate question. Jesus had earlier said, "Let's go over to the other side of the lake." Now, since His men knew His destination, "the other side of the lake," why would they doubt His ability to get them there, even when He was asleep?

> **LEADERSHIP TIP #117**
>
> Anytime you become afraid, consciously rely on Jesus to see you through.

Did you notice how Jesus tied being afraid into not having faith in Him? He pretty well nailed it, didn't he? His point was, since He had the best interests of His followers in His heart, and He had the power to deliver, why would they be afraid? Unless, of course, they didn't totally believe it. Unless they lacked a complete trust in Him.

What a great lesson for His men in that rocking boat. One second, it looked like they would all be going down with the boat. The next second, they could put a full glass of water on the rail, and it wouldn't spill a drop. All at the word of Jesus.

> When fear grips you, how can you consciously rely on Jesus to see you through?

The Gerasene Wild Man

MARK 5:1-20

Shortly after the storm on the lake, Jesus and His men landed on the other side. Unknown to them, a crazed man, perhaps standing in one of the hillside burial caves, was watching as they pulled their boat ashore. Suddenly, the wild man charged toward them, screaming loudly. Jesus' men prob-

> **LEADERSHIP TIP #118**
>
> Regard the needs of your people more highly than financial gain.

ably wanted to jump back into their boat. But, Jesus stood His ground. He quickly determined the man was filled with a "legion" of demons. Yet, in spite of the grip they had on the man, Jesus commanded them to get out. He gave permission for them to enter into a herd of pigs grazing on the cliff above.

Once the demons got into the pigs, the pigs started jumping up and down. Finally, they stampeded down the cliff and drowned in the lake. With that plunge, the owners of the pigs also took a huge financial plunge. Now, how could Jesus justify allowing the demons to enter the pigs? Very simple. Human life was more important than anything else. Besides, those pigs would have been slaughtered in just another week, or two. Their fate had already been determined by their owners.

> In what ways might you be putting financial gain over the needs of your people?

138

AN ANSWER FOR JOHN

MATTHEW 11:1-19

Timing. That was something John the Baptist had lots of "time" to think about in prison. The prison in which King Herod had tossed him. John's disciples had been keeping him updated on reports about Jesus.

LEADERSHIP TIP #119

Patiently wait for God's perfect timing to accomplish His purpose.

However, all the reports seemed to confuse John. When he baptized Jesus, he was sure his distant cousin was the Messiah. Now, he, apparently, wasn't so sure.

John's view of the Messiah was one who would boot the Romans out of the land. He would restore the glory to Israel. Jesus had time to do those things. Yet, He hadn't done either. In fact, Jesus had not even attempted to do either one. So, John sent some of his friends to ask Jesus if He really was the Messiah.

Jesus, perhaps with an understanding smile, told John's friends to report back to him all they had seen Him do. Then, Jesus went on to tell the people how great a person John was. However, in spite of John's greatness, he still needed to wait for God's perfect timing, to do what God wanted to do.

How can you wait on God for His perfect timing when your circumstances have such a grip on you?

139

AN "INCURABLE" WOMAN

LUKE 8:41-48

As Jesus continued to teach the people by the lake, Jairus, an official from the local synagogue, broke through the crowd.
He ran up to Jesus and urgently requested Him to follow him back to his house.

> ### LEADERSHIP TIP #120
>
> Actively do what you can, as a representative of Jesus, to help the "one" in need.

His only child, a 12 year old girl, was dying. He knew that only Jesus could save her. Without wasting a second, Jesus started off alongside the man, with the crowd following close behind.

Before they could get very far, a woman, who had been bleeding for 12 years, pushed her way through the crowd to touch Jesus. She had gone broke hoping the medical world could help her. Now, her only hope was in Jesus. She finally worked her way up through the crowd, and touched His robe.

Instantly, Jesus felt healing energy drain from Him. He stopped, turned around, and asked, "Who touched me?" Quite a question when we consider so many people were pressing around Him. Many people had touched Him. Yet, He was sensitive to the one.

> How can you become more sensitive to the needs of the "one" when so many people are pressing you?

RIDICULE AT JAIRUS'S HOUSE

LUKE 8:49-53

Within seconds after Jesus had healed the woman, a messenger from Jairus's house ran up. He reported to Jairus his little girl had died. It was too late. Can't you imagine the father's heart sinking to the ground? In his anguish, he might have even been fuming at the woman Jesus had cured.

> **LEADERSHIP TIP #121**
>
> Disregard ridicule by seeing your situation through the eyes of Jesus.

Maybe he was even upset with Jesus. Talking with her afterward just took too much time. Why did He do it? Quickly, and perhaps with His hand resting on Jairus's shoulder, Jesus reassured the man. "Just trust me," He said.

Jesus and the crowd arrived at the house, and they were met by the usual loud Jewish crying over the dead. It was actually an act of love from all the neighbors. However, when Jesus told the people, "Stop the weeping. She isn't dead. She's only asleep," their tears of sadness turned into tears of laughter. It was like Jesus didn't have a grip on reality. Anyone could see the girl wasn't breathing. She was obviously dead, not just asleep. Yet, from Jesus' view, she was only sleeping.

1. How can you "just trust" Jesus when all hope has been drained from you?

2. How can you really look through the eyes of Jesus?

141

THE DEAD GIRL GETS UP

LUKE 8:54-56

Jesus walked over to the girl He said was "only asleep." Perhaps He paused for a moment just looking at her lifeless body. He saw no movement of her chest. No breathing at all. She was totally lifeless. Then, He took her by the hand, and quietly said, "Get up, my child."

LEADERSHIP TIP #122

Keep in mind that God is your hope in what appears to be a hopeless situation.

At that very second, air flowed into her lungs. Her heart started beating. She moved a hand. Her eyes blinked. Then, they were open. Life had suddenly flowed from Jesus' live body into a girl's dead body.

She was alive.

What happened that day totally defied God's natural laws of life and death. Yet, God Himself chose for it to happen. Only God has the power, and the reason, to interfere with His own natural laws. What took place that day was a miracle. Interestingly, the girl wasn't weak when she "awoke." She stood up and, apparently, was hungry. It was like, "What's for lunch, mom?"

1. Why doesn't God do miracles today, or does He?

2. How would it affect your reliance on God if He chose not to perform a miracle for you in a desperate need you might have?

142

The Poolside Miracle

John 5:1-9

On one Sabbath day, when Jesus was in Jerusalem, He took a short walk over to the famous Pool of Bethesda. When He entered one of the five patios that surrounded the pool, He saw lots of sick people lying as close to the pool as they could get. Each one wanted to

LEADERSHIP TIP #123

Obey God's word, while relying on His power to bring His results.

be the first into the water when it stirred. They believed the first one in would be healed.

Jesus looked around. Then, His eyes fell on one man. Apparently, from where Jesus stood, the man wasn't showing much enthusiasm for getting into the water. It was like he had lost all hope. Like he was just going through the motions. So, Jesus walked over and asked, "Do you want to be healed?" Maybe Jesus asked the question just to shake the man up a little.

The man shot back a "lame" excuse. Then Jesus commanded him, "Stand up, pick up your sleeping mat, and walk." Not a reasonable thing to say to a man who had been crippled for 38 years. Yet, as the man began to stand up, God's enabling power flowed into him. He stood straight up, totally healed.

In what family situation, or in leading your people, might you have given up hope, and had to rely on God to bring about the results He wanted?

143

RELIGIOUS LEADERS PROTEST

JOHN 5:10-47

Amazing, isn't it? The newly healed man was happily carrying his mat down the road, when the eyes of a few religious leaders caught him. They rushed up to him and said, "You can't work on the Sabbath. It's illegal to carry that sleeping mat."

LEADERSHIP TIP #124

In partnership with Jesus, stay connected to God throughout the day, by talking to Him about everything you see Him doing.

The guy was stunned. He replied, "The man who healed me, said, 'Pick up your sleeping mat and walk.'" Unbelievably, the religious authorities were furious. They demanded to know who told him to do that. They were totally blind to the great miracle that had just happened. Well, the man didn't know who it was. However, Jesus later found him, and talked with him. Then, the man innocently reported back to the religious leaders it was Jesus.

Quickly, the leaders found Jesus. They couldn't wait to lecture Him about healing people on the Sabbath. But, Jesus didn't back down. In their resulting dialogue, Jesus told them, "The Son does only what He sees the Father doing." Then He stung them by saying, "Your approval means nothing to me."

How can you go about your work, wrapped up in what you're doing, and stay tuned in to what God is doing?

144

SENDING OUT THE TWELVE

MARK 6:6-13

The message of love, forgiveness and hope that Jesus' Father had put into His heart had to get out. One problem. If it was totally on Jesus' shoulders, He couldn't do it. Physically, there was just no way He personally could reach the entire world.

LEADERSHIP TIP #125

Team up your people to communicate your message to others.

In fact, He was very aware of how short His present life would be. All part of His Father's plan. So Jesus trained His chosen and loyal men to model and get His message out. In turn, they would train still others, until God's message would eventually reach the entire world.

The time for sending His men out, on a trial run, with His message had now come. So, Jesus teamed them up in twos. He then instructed them what to say and do. Finally, He sent them out. Jesus physically would not be with them. That's why it was important for them to be paired up. Jesus wanted them to help each other. To find strength from each other. He knew well the importance of mutual-effort-companionship.

1. What is the message you want your people to take to others in their world of influence?

2. Who are a few trusted people you can use as your core group in getting the message to still others you are leading?

145

Herod's Foolish Promise

Mark 6:14-29

King Herod Antipas had heard a lot about Jesus. Because of the great things he had heard, the king thought Jesus might even be a resurrected John the Baptist. Herod, of course, was the man who had John's head cut off. Before moving on, let's briefly revisit what happened.

> **LEADERSHIP TIP #126**
>
> Keep in mind that a weak person will save face in front of others, even at the expense of someone else.

John's death was the result of a foolish promise. A promise Herod had given his daughter, Herodias. The girl had danced for Herod and his guests at one of their wild parties. Enthused by her dance, and in a drunken daze, Herod promised the girl he would give her whatever she wanted. Up to half of his kingdom. Well, the girl under the direct orders of her mother, who, by the way, hated John for revealing sin in her life, requested the head of John on a platter.

Now, Herod actually liked John. Yet, he felt compelled to honor his daughter's request, as brainless as that seems. Apparently, the prideful king didn't want to renege in front of all his guests. So, to "save face," he ordered John's head to be cut off.

> In what way can you use this leadership tip to evaluate your people whenever you correct them?

DISCIPLES REPORT TO JESUS

MARK 6:30

When Jesus' men returned from their short-term mission, they were eager to tell Him all that had happened. And, Jesus fully expected them to do so. That's called account-ability. As His men were reporting, no doubt Jesus was content in knowing they were catching on to what He was all about. Oh, they didn't have the same grip on it that Jesus did, but they were coming along.

> **LEADERSHIP TIP 127-A**
>
> Willingly, give an account of your activities to your superiors.
>
> **LEADERSHIP TIP 127-B**
>
> Schedule periodic times for your people to report to you about their activities.

Now, leadership implies structure of some sort, and a chain-of-command. Therefore, leadership requires people to be accountable. Jesus knew that, if people don't answer to their superiors in a chain-of-command, the overall mission can easily be compromised. Even a human leader who appears to report to no one, still must answer to God.

> 1. Why is accountability important?
> 2. Why is verbal accountability needed, even if you want a written report?
> 3. How can you give an accountability report, even if you have no one to whom you're required to report?

147

A Time for Rest

Mark 6:31-32

Jesus' followers were trying to tell Him all the great things that happened on their tour. But, it was a "zoo." At the same time they were talking to their leader, many other people were coming to see Jesus. So many, in fact, He and His men didn't even have time to eat.

LEADERSHIP TIP 128

Schedule periodic times when you and your people can get away together, just for relaxation.

Some of the people might have been coming, hoping Jesus would heal their aching body. Still others, no doubt, were just curious. They all had heard about this tremendous teacher, and about His unbelievable actions. Could He really be as amazing as people were saying? That was what the people wanted to know. To find out for themselves.

Pressed by the crowd, and noticing His men needed time to relax and get refreshed, Jesus said, "Let's go off by ourselves to a quiet place, and rest for awhile." So, they started down the path, leading to one of their boats.

1. Why is physical and mental rest important for your team accomplishing its goals?

2. Why is relaxing together important, along with individual periods of rest and rehabilitation?

BREAKING IT DOWN

LUKE 9:10-17 AND JOHN 6:1-13

The crowd watched Jesus and His men hike down the path to the lake, and set sail. Then, all those people started running alongside the lake, letting more people know where Jesus was heading. By the time Jesus and His tired men had pulled their boat ashore, thousands of

LEADERSHIP TIP #129

Divide your work into smaller, more manageable parts.

people were waiting for them. Compassionately, Jesus walked among them, sharing words from God, and healing those who were sick. His men sat to the side watching, listening...and resting.

Finally, Jesus told His men He wanted to feed the people to give them energy for their long road trip home. The disciples shook their heads. They couldn't see how they could feed over 12,000 people. It would be about that when all the women and children were counted, including 5000 hungry men. After Andrew found a boy with a small lunch, Jesus told His men to divide the huge crowd into more manageable groups of about fifty each. They did it, probably wondering why.

1. Jesus did not yet have the amount of food He needed to feed everyone. So, why did He divide the group?

2. In what ways can you divide your people's workload into more manageable sections?

ONE LUNCH WILL DO

LUKE 9:10-17 AND JOHN 6:1-13

Jesus held the five small barley loaves and two little fish up toward the sky. He thanked His Father. Then, He told His men to bring to Him their large, leather traveling pouches. As they brought them, and held them out, Jesus began breaking the bread and ripping the fish apart. He kept dropping

> **LEADERSHIP TIP #130**
>
> Give all you have over to God, and He will multiply it to accomplish what He has in mind.

the pieces it into the pouches. As each pouch was filled, the disciples walked among the groups, distributing the bread and fish. Then they returned for more.

Imagine the thousands of wide-eyed people, including the twelve disciples and one little boy, when the bread and fish kept multiplying. It just didn't run out. No telling how long this process took. But, before Jesus was through, every person on the grassy hillside had more than enough. This, by the way, is the only miracle Jesus did, outside of His resurrection, that was recorded in all four Gospel accounts.

1. In spite of not being able to rest completely – and that is why Jesus and His men went to the other side – what "refreshing" lesson did Jesus' followers learn?

2. What resources do you have that you still need to give over to God for His purposes?

Praying On A Hill

Matthew 14:22-23 and John 6:14-15

The miracle of multiplying five loaves of bread and two small fish into enough food for everyone, and still have leftovers, did not go unnoticed by the people. No doubt that was all they could talk about in between bites. "Did you see what Jesus did?" "Unbelievable!"

LEADERSHIP #131

Spend longer times in prayer when you are tempted to do something you are not sure God wants you to do.

In fact, the people were so excited, some of them thought Jesus ought to be their king. The idea steamrolled, and everyone got on board. However, Jesus caught wind of what they were talking about. So, He told His men to quietly leave, and set sail for the other side. While they walked down to the lake and climbed into the boat, Jesus discreetly withdrew from the great crowd of eager people. He hiked up the hillside to pray.

Now, why did Jesus suddenly need to pray? Well, wasn't this another temptation from Satan? Couldn't Jesus do more good for the people if He were their king? Very similar to Satan's tactic in the second of the great temptations on the mountain-top. Jesus simply withdrew to talk with His Father.

What might you presently be dealing with, about which you need to spend quality time talking with God to get His thoughts?

WALKING ON WATER

MATTHEW 14:24-36

At the same time Jesus was praying, His men ran into a strong headwind on the lake. It slowed them down to a snail's pace. So, after Jesus had finished praying, He hiked down to the lake. However, He didn't stop at the shoreline. He walked into the lake, then on top of the water. The same man,

LEADERSHIP TIP #132

"Climb out of the boat," keeping your eyes on Jesus, moving toward what He wants you to do.

who hushed a violent storm with a command, now decided to defy gravity. He walked out on the water to meet His team.

His men saw a "ghostlike" figure in the distance approaching, and they were terrified. When Jesus got closer, He told them it was Him. Peter impulsively blurted out for Jesus to tell him to walk to Him. "Come on," Jesus answered. Peter eagerly climbed over the rail and planted his feet on "solid" water. He riveted his eyes on Jesus, and took a few steps. Then, it hit. Peter felt the sting of water in his eyes. He frantically looked away from Jesus and saw danger all around him. Suddenly, he began to sink. Jesus quickly grabbed hold and said, "You don't have much faith, do you? Why did you doubt me?" Good question, Peter. After all, Jesus had just told you to "come."

Peter climbed out of the boat to go where Jesus wanted him to go. What "walking on water" adventure might Jesus have for you, if you just get out of the boat?

ON THE ROAD
WITH JESUS

YEAR THREE

DEDICATED TO
RACHELLE ANTHONY

This section is in honor of my youngest daughter, my second pride and joy, but now tied for first. Rachelle, I discovered, when you were in middle school, you, our spontaneous daughter, you, who never took anything too seriously, you became a "bulldog" in going for something you really wanted. What amazed me then, doesn't anymore. You are one of the most determined people I've ever known in making things happen.

In this section, we move into our third year with Jesus. During this year, Jesus creates a stir in Jerusalem when He stands up in front of a huge crowd, and invites people to come to Him to quench their thirst for a connection to God. Later, He compassionately saves a woman from getting "rocked" to death, and then challenges her to start out fresh, and "sin no more." Jesus ends this year by claiming He is the light of the world.

Rachelle, I can't think of a better year of Jesus' life that reflects the great compassion I see in you for the hurting. You take time to be there for your friends, and others along the way. And, you constantly encourage others to live up to God's higher standard. I see the light of Jesus shining brightly through you with your quick smile, spontaneous spirit, and your enthusiasm for your family and friends.

SOME FOLLOWERS QUIT

JOHN 6:53-71

One day, after walking on water, Jesus was teaching in the Capernaum synagogue. "I tell you the truth," He said, "unless you eat the flesh of the Son of Man and drink his blood, you have no life in you."

LEADERSHIP TIP #133

Expect the less committed among your people to lose heart in moments of difficulty.

Well, that shook up His listeners. They just could not figure it out. So, some of His disciples deserted Him. Sure, it was hard to understand. But, why did they just pack up and leave when He said something that didn't set well? Anyone who knew Jesus at all understood He wasn't telling His followers to become cannibals.

Jesus sadly gazed at the backs of many of His "followers" disappearing down the road. After a minute, or so, He turned to His twelve, and asked, "Are you leaving, too?" Peter put it bluntly, speaking for the rest of the team. "Lord," he said, "to whom would we go? You alone have the words that give eternal life. We believe them, and we know you are the Holy One of God." Then, after hearing their pledge of loyalty, Jesus predicted that even one of them would eventually betray Him.

Before you get into a major situation, how might you be able to determine who among the people you lead are the less committed?

155

WHAT DEFILES A PERSON

MARK 7:14-23

Jesus' followers had just watched some people walk out on Him. Soon after, His team was tested again. This time, by what Jesus said about eating what they considered to be "unclean" food. Now, regardless of one's view about the "clean" and "unclean" food listed in Leviticus

LEADERSHIP TIP #134

Take time each day to purify your thoughts and attitudes with God's Word.

11, this teaching of Jesus is clear. When Jesus and His men entered a house, they asked Him about what He had just said. "You are not defiled," Jesus explained, "by what you eat; you are defiled by what you say and do!"

Then, Jesus gave His team a list of things that do defile a person spiritually. Why? Because, He said, they come out of the heart: Evil thoughts, sexual immorality, theft, murder, adultery, greed, wickedness, deceit, eagerness for lustful pleasure, envy, slander, and pride. Not an exhaustive list, but it was a start. Jesus' idea was these defile a person because they are a result of a person being out of fellowship with God.

1. Why does a muddy glass of water eventually become pure as pure water keeps running into it?

2. How can the pure word of God coming into your mind be likened to pure water running into a glass of muddy water?

Throwing Bread to Dogs

Mark 7:24-30

Jesus took His men for a short trip, up to the towns of Tyre and Sidon. They were northwest of Nazareth, on the shore of the Mediterranean Sea. Perhaps Jesus wanted to give His men more in-depth training. Or, maybe He just wanted to take His message to the Gentiles. Whatever His motive, as they were walking along a road, a Gentile woman ran up and fell at Jesus' feet. She begged Him to cast demons out of her daughter.

LEADERSHIP TIP #135

Use provocative statements, every now and then, to challenge the thinking of your people.

For some reason, Jesus decided to test her faith. He said, "First, I should help my own family, the Jews. It isn't right to take the bread of the children and throw it to dogs."

The woman didn't flinch at the word, "dogs." She came right back. "That's true, Lord," she said, "but even the dogs under the table are given crumbs from the children's plate." Now, that got to Jesus. You can almost see Him smiling, and nodding to the feisty woman. "Good answer," He said, "and because you have answered so well, I have healed your daughter."

What can you say to those you lead to get them to take what they're doing to a higher level?

157

LEAVING THE CROWD BEHIND

MARK 7:31-37

After Jesus and His men left Tyre and Sidon, some people brought a deaf man to Jesus, a man who also had a speech impediment. The people were looking for Jesus to heal him.

However, instead of healing the man on the spot, Jesus led him away from all the people. He wanted to go to a more private place. So, when they got out on an isolated road, Jesus put His fingers in the man's ears. Then, He pulled them out, spit on His fingers, and touched the man's tongue with the spittle. Spittle, by the way, was considered to have healing qualities.

> **LEADERSHIP TIP #136**
>
> Meet the needs of others, including those you lead, as privately as possible.

Jesus looked up and said, "Be open." Instantly, the man could hear perfectly, and he could also speak clearly. No speech impediment at all. Strangely, right after Jesus restored the man's hearing, He told the crowd, who had gathered, not to spread the word about what He had just done. However, they were "deaf" to what He said. They couldn't stop talking about it.

1. Why did Jesus use His spittle when He didn't need to use it to heal the man?

2. Why did Jesus tell the crowd not to tell others what He did when His whole idea was to reach others?

FEEDING OVER 4000 GENTILES

MARK 8:1-9

Talk about déjà vu. A few days after Jesus had healed the deaf man, He was teaching a crowd of thousands of Gentiles when they ran out of food. He turned to His disciples, and told them He wanted to feed everyone.

> **LEADERSHIP TIP #137**
>
> Schedule a "reflection break" every now and then, just to chew on some of the things you have seen God do.

Once again, His men looked only for stores in the area to supply the food. There weren't any. And, there was no food growing in the wilderness, either. Hey, it wasn't that long ago Jesus fed thousands of Jews with a boy's sack lunch. His men must have been suffering from a short term memory loss.

Jesus asked His followers how many loaves of bread they had between them. "Seven," was their answer. You could almost see Jesus smiling when He indicated that would be enough. He blessed the bread. Then He started breaking the loaves and handing His men the pieces to give out to the people. Like before, the bread kept multiplying. They also found a few fish, and Jesus multiplied the fish, too.

> 1. In leading your people, what is the value of taking "reflection breaks" to relect on God's activity?
>
> 2. How might you incorporate such a break into your people's schedule?

The Leaven of Pharisees

MARK 8:13-21

Some Pharisees came to challenge Jesus. They wanted Him to give them a sign to prove who He was. Jesus just shook His head in amazement at their constant testing of Him. He turned and walked away. Then, He and His men climbed into a boat to cross the lake. However, on the

> **LEADERSHIP TIP #138**
>
> Use what is on the mind of someone else to draw his attention to a truth, or value, you want to communicate.

way over, the hungry disciples suddenly panicked. They realized they hadn't brought enough bread. They had only one loaf between thirteen hungry men.

"Beware of the yeast of the Pharisees and of Herod," Jesus warned, seemingly coming out of nowhere. His disciples responded with twelve blank stares. So, Jesus asked, "Why are you so worried about food? Won't you ever learn or understand?" Again, blank stares. "Don't you remember anything at all?" Then, Jesus helped His men remember the miraculous feeding of both the Jews and the Gentiles.

His point? If Jesus could take care of thousands of people with just a few loaves, why couldn't He take care of His twelve men with just one loaf?

> What are things your people tend to think about the most, and how can you use their thoughts to teach them truths?

HEALING IN STAGES

MARK 8:22-26

No sooner had Jesus and His men landed on the other side of the lake, some villagers brought a blind man for Him to heal. However, Jesus didn't heal the man on the spot. Instead, He took him by the hand, and led him out of the village. Once outside, He spit on the man's eyes. The man didn't see it coming.

> **LEADERSHIP TIP #139**
>
> When things are going slowly, keep in mind that God sometimes chooses to work in both natural ways, and progressive stages.

"Can you see anything?" Jesus asked. "Yes, but not very clearly. It just looks like a lot of trees walking around." Now, I know what you're thinking. *Hey, how can he see anything clearly? He has spit in his eyes.* Well, that wasn't the reason. God had a purpose in this multi-stage healing. Next, Jesus lifted His hands, and put them on the man's eyes. Then, slowly, He took His hands away. The man stared intently. Yes, he could see. His sight was completely restored. Surprisingly, Jesus told the man to go home, but not through the village.

1. What does Jesus' use of His spittle tell us about how God often works?

2. Why did Jesus heal the man in stages rather than right away, and how might God be working in stages in what He has called you to do?

THE WRONG TIME

JOHN 7:1-10

The hostility of the religious leaders was mounting fast against Jesus down south, in Judea. Because of that, He had been staying up north in Galilee, walking from village to village, bringing people His message.

LEADERSHIP TIP #140

Ask God to help you clearly think through what is the most strategic time for you to accomplish what He wants you to do.

However, the time for the Jewish Feast of the Tabernacles in Jerusalem was approaching. Most people would be making the journey south, including His own family. Now, at this point in Jesus' outreach, His own brothers did not believe in Him as the Messiah. So, as brothers like to taunt one another, they mockingly urged Jesus to go to the festival to make a big splash.

Another man might have done just what his brothers were trying to get Him to do. Just to prove he was the real thing. To prove them wrong. However, Jesus knew going at that time was not what His Father wanted Him to do. "This is not the right time for me to go," He answered, without missing a beat. Jesus stuck to what He believed was best. And, as His family was on the road heading south, He stood, waving goodbye to them.

What steps will you take to know what is God's strategic time for you to do something?

The Right Time

John 7:11-29

Soon after Jesus' brothers had set out for Jerusalem, most likely, in a caravan with other travelers, Jesus and His men started out on the same road heading south. They reached Jerusalem about the midway point of the festival. It was the exact time Jesus had planned. His mid-feast arrival

> **LEADERSHIP TIP #141**
>
> Prayerfully plan, then implement that plan to accomplish what God wants you to do.

caught the religious leaders off guard. Because Jesus had waited until His Father's strategic time to go to the festival, the religious leaders had relaxed their lookout for Him. So, Jesus and His men slipped into the city, relatively unnoticed.

Jesus started teaching in the temple courts without any opposition. However, He soon found that public opinion was divided on Him. Some people didn't think He was the Messiah. Others asked, "Would you expect the Messiah to do more miraculous signs than this man has done?"

In a short time, once again, Jesus was debating the religious leaders. Still, they were simply no match for Him. That's why, all the more, they wanted to kill the Man from Galilee.

> What is the balance between making your plans, and getting your leading from God?

163

The Invisible Shield

JOHN 7:30

Jesus kept teaching at the festival in spite of the increased hostility of the religious leaders. He was on their turf, yet He boldly took the attack to them, never giving an inch.

> **LEADERSHIP TIP #142**
>
> Rely on God to protect you to accomplish His assignment for you.

Now, it wasn't because the Pharisees had backed down that Jesus was able to keep teaching. In fact, it was just the opposite.

The angry Pharisees had even upped their attacks by sending the temple police out to arrest Him. However, each time the officers went to bring Jesus in, they returned empty-handed.

The officers would walk up to where Jesus was surrounded by a group of eager listeners. Then, unexplainably, they would get caught up in what Jesus was saying, just like everyone else. Each time, they reported back to the temple authorities empty-handed. It was like an invisible shield was protecting Jesus. His "time" simply had not yet come.

1. How does your walking in God's timing help you to live in the present tense?

2. In what ways have you seen God's timing in working with your people?

A QUENCHER FOR THIRST

JOHN 7:37-39

On each day of the festival, a priest walked out to the Pool of Siloam, just outside the city wall. He gathered about two pints of water in a golden pitcher. Then he paraded back through the streets to the temple, as the people looked on. At the temple, while he poured the water over the altar,

> **LEADERSHIP TIP #143**
>
> Be a conduit for the life-giving water of Jesus to flow to the people you lead.

the people recited Isaiah 12:3. "With joy you will draw water from the well of salvation." That was repeated day after day.

Then, on the last, and climatic day of the festival, the priest, carrying the water back from the pool, marched around the altar seven times before pouring out the water. That symbolized marching seven times around the walls of Jericho before the walls came crashing to the ground. Just as the priest was pouring out the water on that last day, Jesus went into action. He might have first climbed up on a large stone block, and cupped His hands around His mouth. Then, He shouted to the huge crowd, "If any one thirsts, let him come to me!" Did that ever grab their attention!

1. What kind of thirst was Jesus talking about?

2. How can you create a thirst in your people for Jesus?

Tossing the First Rock

John 8:1-11

The next day, Jesus walked into the Temple complex and a crowd quickly gathered. The religious leaders were ready and waiting for Him. In an attempt to get an official charge against Jesus, they dragged a woman to Him who they had just trapped in adultery. Pushing their way through the crowd,

> **LEADERSHIP TIP #144**
>
> Help people, who are quick to judge others, understand we all fall short of God's standard.

they threw her down on the dusty pavement in front of Jesus. "The Law of Moses says to stone her," they said, with a defiant glare. "What do you say?"

They figured, because of Jesus' well-known compassion, He would say to let her go. Were they ever caught off guard. Instead of answering, Jesus just stooped down and used His finger to scribble something in the dust. Then He slowly rose to His feet, and came back at her accusers, in a calm, calculating tone. "All right," He said, "stone her. But let those who have never sinned throw the first stones!"

Jesus stooped again to scribble in the dust. As He wrote, one by one, the accusers, from the oldest to the youngest, dropped the rocks from their hands. They silently slipped off.

How can you help your people be more forgiving of each other?

SIN NO MORE

JOHN 8:1-11

The last of the woman's accusers walked off, leaving rocks scattered over the pavement. Jesus then straightened up, and looked around the area. The woman was still on the pavement at His feet.

LEADERSHIP TIP #145

Encourage a person, when he has done wrong, to start living on a higher plane of life.

Perhaps He bent over and helped her up, as He asked, "Where are your accusers? Didn't even one of them condemn you?" "No, Lord," she replied. What a relief it must have been for the disgraced woman when she saw the warm smile on Jesus' face, then heard His words, "Neither do I."

Interestingly, Jesus did not just want to help the woman know she was loved by God. He did not just want to let her know God had forgiven her. He wanted even more for her. He wanted her to experience the higher level of life God still had in store for her. So, He gave her a challenge to motivate her to take positive steps. Steps to leave her immorality behind. Steps to start a new life. Looking deep into her eyes, He lifted her hopes with the words, "Go, and sin no more."

When a person you're leading blows it, how can you help him experience God's forgiveness as well as yours? Also, how can you encourage him to take positive steps to move forward?

THE LIGHT OF THE WORLD

JOHN 8:12

The temple was the turf on which Jesus battled the religious leaders. In fact, they carried on a running debate. Now, you would have thought the temple authorities would have welcomed Jesus with open arms. Not so.

> ## LEADERSHIP TIP #146
>
> Each day, be sure the "light of the world" is the light shining through you to the people you lead.

The Pharisees had been teaching the people legalism. People had to meticulously obey insignificant rules to experience God. Rules, by the way, the Pharisees and their cohorts themselves had developed. Then Jesus came along, and shouted out His invitation in the temple the day before, "If anyone is thirsty, let him come to me."

Now, as the crowd watched a forgiven and new woman walk away, Jesus struck another raw nerve in the religious leaders. He boldly told the onlookers, "I am the light of the world. If you follow me, you won't be stumbling through the darkness, because you will have the light that leads to life."

1. The word for "light" Jesus used to describe Himself was the Greek word meaning light from its own source, like the sun. Why did Jesus use that word when God is the only light from its own source?

2. What steps can you take to make sure you have the "light" of Jesus in you?

A Strategic Hiding

JOHN 8:13-59

Visitors to the temple stood by, listening to every word of the battle of the minds between Jesus and the Pharisees. Of course, some of the onlookers had already made up their own mind about Jesus. Others were still trying to sort it all out. It shocked some of the people when,

LEADERSHIP TIP #147

Avoid unnecessary challenges.

Jesus, driving home a point of who He was, said that He was superior in rank to even the revered Abraham. "The truth is," He claimed, "I existed before Abraham was even born!"

Even the people who were fairly open-minded had a hard time with that one. Abraham had been dead a long time. They even knew where their patriarch was buried. Now, there in front of them, stood a rugged looking, young carpenter who claimed He had existed before Abraham was even born. That was too much for the average I.Q. to grasp. It just didn't make sense.

Most likely, spurred on by the religious leaders, a few people evolved into an angry mob. They wanted to stone Jesus for what they considered to be outright blasphemy. Jesus knew His time had not yet come. So, He hid Himself from the mob. Later, He quietly slipped out of the temple.

If Jesus knew He was under the protection of His Father to complete His mission, why did He choose to hide Himself?

169

A MAN'S BLINDNESS

JOHN 9:1-3

Jesus had got away from the crowd who wanted to kill Him in the temple. Now, He and His men were openly walking along a road, coming up on a man who had been born blind. The man had never visibly seen anything. He just lived in a dark world of sounds and touches. His only way to "make a

> **LEADERSHIP TIP #148**
>
> Keep in mind that some sickness is for the glory of God to shine through the person.

living" was to sit by the side of the road, and beg for money. That didn't do a lot for his self-worth.

Now, sickness, in Jesus' day, was thought to be the result of a person's sins. In some cases, if it was a sickness from birth, it could be the result of his parent's sins. So, one of Jesus' men, with his inquiring mind in full gear, asked his leader, "Why was this man born blind? Was it a result of his own sins or those of his parents?"

Jesus' reply had to leave His men wondering. "It was not because of his sins or his parents' sins," Jesus answered. "He was born blind so the power of God could be seen in him." Jesus was about to show His men exactly what He meant.

> Many sicknesses are the result of the sin of poor health choices, choices apart from God's health laws, as well as other factors. How can you know when a person has become sick mainly for God's glory?

HEALING A BLIND MAN

JOHN 9:10-41

Jesus grabbed some dirt, spit on it, and stirred it around. Then, as He spread the "salve" on the blind man's eyes, He told him to wash it off in the Pool of Siloam. The man managed to walk to the pool, and, as he stooped down to wash his eyes, he could see for the first time in his life. He never thought he would "see" that day.

LEADERSHIP TIP #149

Help your people become open-minded about Jesus.

When the religious leaders heard about the man being healed, they quickly came knocking. Why? It happened on the Sabbath. Well, the man told them what Jesus had done for him. However, the close-minded religious leaders couldn't accept what the man said. A common "sinner" like Jesus could never have given the man sight.

The man thought it strange the leaders were so opposed to Jesus. He said, "God doesn't listen to sinners, but He is ready to hear those who worship Him and do His will. Never since the world began has anyone been able to open the eyes of someone born blind. If this man were not from God, He couldn't do it." Later, because the former blind man said he believed in Jesus, he was black-balled from the synagogue.

How will you help your people become open-minded about Jesus?

171

A WARNING ABOUT SATAN

JOHN 10:10

Winter was approaching, and in the fields, shepherds were herding their sheep into pens for their protection. It might have been when Jesus, and the crowd following Him, were walking by one of those pens that He turned and grabbed their attention. He said that He Himself was the gate for the sheep to walk through to safety. Every-

LEADERSHIP TIP #150

Keep on your guard for Satan's attempts to gradually destroy the life God has designed for you, as well as what God has designed for the people you lead.

one scratched their heads a little, so Jesus detailed it out a bit. To emphasize how He came to give new life to His "sheep," He contrasted His role to Satan's role.

He described Satan as a thief who would dig under the wall of a sheep pen to get in to steal the sheep. "The thief's purpose," He said, "is to steal and kill and destroy." It's interesting, the word "destroy" means to "utterly annihilate." Jesus was saying that's exactly what Satan was out to do. If the thief couldn't get the "sheep" for himself, he would totally wipe them out. Not a very nice guy. Extreme "life and death" matters, Jesus felt, called for extreme illustrations.

How can you help your people be alert to Satan's ways, when those people might not even think Satan exists?

A LIFE OVERFLOWING

JOHN 10:10

Walking by that sheep pen, followed by a crowd of eager listeners, Jesus had just set the stage for one of His most powerful, and attractive teachings. First, He warned His followers that Satan was out to totally destroy them anyway he could.

LEADERSHIP TIP #151

"Plug" totally into Jesus as the only source for your life, and, daily, commit yourself to His purpose for you.

Then He boldly claimed, perhaps pointing to Himself with both hands, "I came that you may have life, and have it more abundantly." Interestingly, the Greek word Jesus used for "abundantly" means to be "full to the brim, and running over." That was the quality of life He told the people He came to give. A life overflowing.

Jesus, of course, spelled out what that overflowing life was with many of His other teachings. He also promised that anyone, who was truly repentant of their sins, could experience that life by joining up with Him. Take a moment to imagine the greatest quality of life possible. Now, here's what Jesus was saying. The quality of life He came to give is far superior to anything you could have just seen in your mind's eye.

An electric lamp must plug into an electrical outlet for it to function properly. What does it mean to "plug" into Jesus, and to, daily, commit yourself to His purpose for you?

173

THE GOOD SHEPHERD

JOHN 10:11-13

Jesus and His followers might have paused for a few minutes on the roadside, watching a hired hand work the sheep in the nearby field. It was clear the man wasn't going about his work as enthusiastically as the owner of the sheep. Then, perhaps with a smile, Jesus went

LEADERSHIP TIP #152

Place the good of the people you lead ahead of your own good.

on to explain the difference between a hired hand and a true-to-the-heart shepherd. He said the hired hand would run away when a wolf came prowling. He wasn't committed. The shepherd, on the other hand, would be willing to even lay down his life for his sheep. He would fight the wolf to the death.

Then, Jesus claimed, "I am the good shepherd; I know my own sheep, and they know me, just as my Father knows me and I know the Father. And I lay down my life for the sheep. I have other sheep, too, that are not in this sheepfold. I must bring them also, and they will listen to my voice; and there will be one flock with one shepherd." In that one statement, Jesus let His followers know His future. By putting the good of His followers ahead of Himself, He would eventually give up His life. Gladly give it up. Out of love and commitment.

In what ways do you need to work at putting the good of your people ahead of your own good, perhaps even with some of your policies?

174

ON THE ROAD
WITH JESUS

YEAR FOUR

DEDICATED TO
PEGGY NEAL

This section is in honor of my honey, my wife, and my "walking through life" partner. Believe me, Peggy, there is absolutely no year in Jesus' life that best reflects what I see in you every single day.

In this section, we move into our fourth and final year going "on the road" with Jesus. It's showdown time, and Jesus doesn't back off from it. He faces down God's enemies. Sure, they finally "get Him." However, little did they know, He wouldn't stay down. Instead, Jesus uses His death on the cross as a springboard for His resurrection. And, with His rising from the tomb, He brings new life to everyone He touches.

Peggy, if there ever was a person who caught what Jesus was all about, dying to self, and bringing new life to others, you're the person. I saw it in how you willingly gave up yourself to care for your parents, and my mom, when all three came to live with us, at different times, in the sunset years of their lives. I see it in how you're always there for our daughers, grandkids, and for me. I see it in how your enthusiasm for life causes other people to get a little more enthused. Ya know, I didn't marry my best friend. But, in our years together, going from one adventure to another, you have become better than a best friend to me. I'm not into syrupy lingo, as you know, but you really are my "soul-mate." You're a life-giver!

TWO KEY QUESTIONS

MATTHEW 16:13-20

How did Jesus expect His followers to start up a conversation about Him? Well, Jesus Himself gave them a great strategy for doing it. One day, He and His men were hiking through the region of Caesarea Philippi.

LEADERSHIP TIP #153

Start a conversation about Jesus by asking what other people think of Him. Then, ask the person what he personally thinks about Jesus.

They were high on a terrace overlooking a fertile valley, directly north of the Sea of Galilee. He casually turned to His men, and asked, "Who do people say the Son of Man is?" "John the Baptist," one of them replied. "Elijah," came another. One disciple even answered, "Jeremiah." Jesus listened carefully, perhaps nodding at each answer. Then, still in a relaxed manner, yet, perhaps stopping and looking directly at them, He asked, "Who do you say I am?" Peter blurted out, "You are the Messiah, the Son of the Living God."

What a brilliant indirect way to get to the real issue. Jesus knew most people don't mind telling what other people are thinking. It isn't threatening to them. Then, once they get into the flow of things, it's easier to talk about what they think.

Who might you use this strategy on within the next couple of days?

177

REBUKING PETER

MARK 8:32-33

Later, Jesus would teach His followers to go to a person privately when they found a fault that needed to be addressed. However, in this episode, Jesus let Peter have it in front of all of his friends, the rest of the disciples. Now, why did Jesus correct him so publicly?

LEADERSHIP TIP #154

Rebuke someone in front of others only when all the people are wrongly thinking the same thing; otherwise, rebuke someone individually, and in private.

High on that terrace in Caesarea Philippi, right after Peter boldly told his leader he knew He was the Messiah, Jesus started telling His men the terrible things that were going to happen to Him in Jerusalem. Yes, He would be killed. However, three days later, He would come back to life. Apparently, all Peter heard was the "killed" part. Probably vigorously shaking his head, he quickly took Jesus aside and reprimanded Him for saying such things.

As Peter was "correcting" his friend, Jesus glanced over at the rest of the disciples. Then He rebuked Peter, in front of them all. Now, what did Jesus see in the rest of His men? Most likely, He knew they were thinking the same thing Peter was.

Why is it normally better to correct a person in private, just between that person and you?

The New Earth Viewpoint

MATTHEW 16:21-26

Jesus now made it clear why He had rebuked Peter. "You are seeing things," He said, "merely from a human point of view, and not from God's." Yet, it wasn't just Peter. It was pretty much all of His men. They all needed the same correction.

LEADERSHIP TIP #155

Develop a New Earth viewpoint through which you will see every situation.

"What does it profit a man," Jesus asked, "if he gain the whole world, and, yet, lose his soul?" He was telling His followers not to be caught up in a world viewpoint that thnks only about the present. A world viewpoint that says, "More material things make life better." It was like Jesus was thinking ahead to the 21st century. He could see His followers living with one foot in the world and one foot in the Kingdom. He knew it couldn't be done. Not in a pleasing way to God.

Jesus was coaching His team to think with a New Earth viewpoint. To think of the new world coming, and what life will be like in that world. Then, with that New Earth viewpoint, to also enjoy the wonders of this present world in fellowship with God, and with each other. Just like He was doing.

1. What can you do to develop a New Earth viewpoint?

2. How can you help your people also have a New Earth viewpoint?

THE MOUNTAIN EXPERIENCE

MATTHEW 17:1-13

The mountain in this episode was probably the snow-capped, Mount Hermon. It was just a few miles north of where Jesus and His men had been hiking. It was so tall it could be seen all the way from the Dead Sea, over 100 miles to the south.

LEADERSHIP TIP #156

In facing difficulties, fix your mind on the body you will one day have in close fellowship with Jesus Himself.

Jesus left nine of His men at the base of the mountain. Then, He took Peter, James and John on the climb with Him up the steep slope. The four men finally reached a plateau overlooking the valley below. In the next few minutes, as Jesus was praying a few feet away from His friends, they were awestruck. Jesus' inner godly radiance broke through His flesh. They saw Him actually glowing.

Suddenly, two great men of the Old Testament era, Moses and Elijah, appeared. They were very much alive, and standing next to Jesus. For the next few minutes, they encouraged Him for His challenging road ahead. Perhaps, they told Him to keep His mind on the radiance He would, once again, have on the New Earth.

1. How can you fix your mind on being in the presence of Jesus?

2. How can that image fixed in your mind help get you through tough times in this world?

CURING AN EPILEPTIC

MARK 9:14-29

The nine disciples who had stayed at the foot of the mountain, as a crowd gathered, ended up arguing with some religious leaders. As Jesus and His friends came down off the mountain, He saw what was going on. So, when the crowd rushed up to welcome Him back, Jesus asked, "What

LEADERSHIP TIP #157

Only vital, believing, prayer will help you to do the tough things God has called you to do.

was all the arguing about?" A man stepped forward out of the crowd and explained he had asked Jesus' disciples to cure his epileptic son, but they couldn't.

Jesus must have frowned and shook His head when He said, "You faithless people. How long must I be with you until you believe? Bring the boy to me."

Just as the father was leading the boy to Jesus, an evil spirit tossed him on the ground into a wild convulsion. The father begged Jesus, "Do something, if you can!" "If I can," Jesus answered, "Anything is possible if a person believes." Then Jesus healed the boy. He later explained to His followers, "This kind can be cast out only by prayer."

How can you develop belief that God will answer your prayer requests? (Think in terms of how a child develops into an Olympic champion.)

181

HIS APPROACHING DEATH

LUKE 9:43-45

The people at the base of the mountain were wild over what they just saw. All they could talk about was what Jesus had just done Jesus for the epileptic boy. As the people were retelling it over and over again, Jesus quietly motioned for His men to join Him off to the side.

Then, with everything so positive all around Him,

> ## LEADERSHIP TIP #158
>
> Keep explaining upcoming events to your people, so that, in spite of their present lack of understanding, they will eventually grasp what you're saying.

Jesus told them, again, of His coming death. This time He gave more details. He made it clear He would be betrayed. That could only mean one thing. One of His own "loyal" followers would do it, someone who appeared to have His trust.

Yet, to Jesus' team, He looked invincible. Even if His enemies did make an attempt on His life, how would the people of the land allow it? Their leader was so popular. Jesus' warning just didn't make sense to His men. They were a trusted group of followers that included a man named Judas Iscariot. He was the disciple who kept their money bag.

1. Why did Jesus keep explaining what was going to happen to Him, when He knew it was just going over the heads of His followers?

2. What can you do to keep your people informed of upcoming events that will affect them?

PAYING THE TAX

MATTHEW 17:24-27

Jesus, with His entourage, left the Mount Hermon area, and walked back to Capernaum, their headquarters. Just as they set foot in town, a tax-collector took Peter aside, and asked him if Jesus had paid the required temple tax.

LEADERSHIP TIP #159

Help your people identify with you by doing some things you aren't really required to do.

Peter mistakenly said He did, but when he talked to Jesus about it, Peter got the impression Jesus didn't even think the tax applied to Him. However, to avoid "rocking the boat," Jesus told Peter to go down to the lake and throw in a line. Then, perhaps with a knowing grin, He told the fisherman, "Open the mouth of the first fish you catch, and you will find a coin. Take it and pay the temple tax for both of us."

Hey, with all the fish in the lake, how did Jesus know the first one Peter would catch would have a coin in its mouth? Well, Peter knew better than to question His leader. Time and time again, what Jesus said, as incredible as it sometimes sounded, proved to be true. So, Peter went, and he found the coin in the first fish's mouth. Just like Jesus said He would.

What are two things you can do with your people that are good, but are not required for you to do?

183

WHO IS THE GREATEST?

LUKE 9:46-48

It happens on most teams, and it definitely happened on the "greatest" team ever assembled. A clash of egos. One day, several of Jesus' men were arguing with each other about who was the greatest among them. "Hey, I'm greater than you!" "Oh sure you are.

> **LEADERSHIP TIP #160**
>
> Help your people understand your definition of greatness.

Well, compared to me, you're nothing but a little kid." Okay, maybe their words were different, but their attitudes were the same. Ego against ego.

Jesus probably shook His head from side to side in amazement as He walked over to a little child. He took him by the hand, and led him back to His men. "Whoever welcomes this little child," He said, "welcomes me, and whoever welcomes me welcomes the one who sent me." Then He hit home with the words, "Whoever is the least among you is the greatest."

The little kid probably didn't understand what was going on. However, what Jesus said helped His men get a better grip on how He defined greatness. At least, for the moment.

1. How do you define greatness?

2. What object lesson can you give to your people to help them understand your definition of greatness?

Dealing With a Wrongdoer

Matthew 18:15-17

Jesus gave His followers three practical steps for dealing with a wrongdoer. Now, although the context of these steps are for dealing with a fellow Christian, let's look at how they would apply to anyone in any organization.

> **LEADERSHIP TIP #161**
>
> Use the three steps in Matthew 18 to deal, individually, with any of your people who are out of line.

Step 1. By yourself, and in private, go to the person you feel has done wrong. Explain how you see it. If the person is truly repentant, and will change, you can skip the next two steps. However, if the person does not respond well, go on to Step 2.

Step 2. With one or two others in your organization who agree with you, go to the person again, with all of you explaining how you feel. If the person responds well, you can stop here. If he doesn't go on to Step 3.

Step 3. Bring the person before your entire organization, and explain the problem. If the person still does not respond well, cut him off from any fellowship with the group in an effort to bring him to his senses.

> Think through a situation in which you would use the three steps Jesus taught His followers.

185

490TH DEGREE FORGIVENESS

MATTHEW 18:21-22

As Jesus was instructing His men about dealing with wrong-doers, Peter popped up, "How many times should I forgive someone who sins against me? Seven times?" Peter might have been having a problem with one of his buddies, so this was a very practical question.

LEADERSHIP TIP #162

Keep on infinitely forgiving the person the same offense.

In fact, the phrase he used for "sins against me" implied it was the same offense, time and time again.

Peter was even being generous with the number "seven." You see, the rabbis taught if you forgave a person three times for the same offense, that would be noble. Well, Peter took it to the next level, and went for the perfect number seven. So, you can imagine how shocked he was when Jesus replied, perhaps shaking His head, "No, not seven," and, then with a nod, "but seven times seven."

Now, did Jesus really mean to count up to 490 times, then lower the boom on the person? No. He was telling Peter to keep forgiving as long as the person did the offense. Jesus taught His people to take forgiveness to the 490th degree. A new way of forgiving, for a new way of living.

How can you keep forgiving another person, and how can you teach your people to do the same?

THE UNFORGIVING SERVANT

MATTHEW 18:23-35

Jesus continued His lesson on the new kind of forgiveness by telling His men a story. It was about a servant who owed his master, the king, millions of dollars. The king was ready to throw the man and his entire family into prison. However, at the begging of the servant, the king had a change of heart. He decided to forgive the man the entire debt. The ultimate pardon.

LEADERSHIP TIP #163

Enthusiastically, pass on to the people you lead the same forgiveness God has given you.

The elated servant immediately went to one of his fellow workers who owed him a few thousand dollars, and demanded full payment, on the spot. When his fellow servant was not able to pay, the forgiven servant angrily had the man thrown into jail. Well, the king was furious when he heard, through the grapevine, what the servant did. So, he called the man back, withdrew his forgiveness of the debt, and tossed him into prison until he repaid the entire millions of dollars. Then, Jesus said, "That's what my heavenly Father will do to you if you refuse to forgive your brothers and sisters in your heart." Wow. A pretty tough teaching. But, for a reason.

How do you know God is absolutely serious about you forgiving the people you lead of their wrongdoings?

The "No Revenge" Policy

LUKE 9:51-56

Jesus knew His death was fast approaching. But, instead of running from it, He was on the road to Jerusalem to meet His destiny head on. How-ever, on the way, He had lots of stops to make. At least one of them would take them through Sa-maria, where He and His

> **LEADERSHIP TIP #164**
>
> Without taking revenge, walk away from someone who mistreats you.

men needed to overnight. That would be tough. You see, the "hobby" for most Samaritans was harrassing Jews traveling through their region. Jesus sent a few men on ahead to make arrangements, but they were rudely turned away. When the men reported back to Jesus, James and John, overheard. The two brothers got fired up with anger.

"Lord," they said, red-faced and rushing up to Jesus, "should we order down fire out of heaven to burn them up?" They thought any kind of revenge would have been too soft. The two brothers must have been stunned when Jesus rebuked them. Instead of taking a "pound of flesh," Jesus led His men to a different Samaritan village where they would be more welcome. It might have even been the one in which the wom-an Jesus had met at the well, and her friends, lived.

> How can you walk away from a person mistreating you without taking revenge, and without other people seeing you as a coward, or, can you?

SENDING OUT THE SEVENTY-TWO – PART 1

SPECIAL ASSIGNMENTS

LUKE 10:1-16

Walking along the hole-riddled, dirt roads, and in the villages where they stayed, Jesus had been teaching more people than just the twelve about life in God's Kingdom. So, before He and His twelve followers reached Jerusalem, He decided to give another seventy-two of His followers "on the job" training. Jesus wanted them to get this experience before He was crucified.

> **LEADERSHIP TIP #165**
>
> Give your people special assignments that represent you, along with the specific instructions on how to carry out each assignment.

Now, on this and the next two pages, we'll look at three leadership tips from the instructions Jesus gave to the seventy-two, as well as *how* He gave those instructions. To catch the overall picture, it will be best to read the entire account out of your Bible. Then, come on back and let's look at the leadership tips, one by one.

1. When is it time to give your people assignments that will stretch them in carrying out your work?

2. Why is it important to give your people specific instructions for carrying out each assignment?

SENDING OUT THE SEVENTY-TWO – PART 2

ENCOURAGEMENT

LUKE 10:1

Jesus sent His seventy-two ambassadors "ahead in pairs to all the towns and places He planned to visit." Okay, they were to prepare the way. But, why send them out two by two? Why didn't Jesus send His seventy-two member team out individually to seventy-two different areas? Why

> **LEADERSHIP TIP #166**
>
> Pair up your people to encourage each other in tackling your special assignments for them.

limit them to just thirty-six areas in teams of two? One simple reason...encouragement. He wanted them to be encouraged.

Hey, who doesn't need a little cheering section once in awhile? Jesus knew that even His owns followers would need it. Especially when they trekked into unfamiliar towns and regions. Well, why not just give each of them a puppy dog for encouragement? Then, they could cover more territory. Although pets are nice, the kind of encouragement Jesus knew His men would need was in the form of words and actions. Words and actions packaged in another person. It was a wise and strategic move, by a wise and strategic leader.

> How will you know who to pair up with whom when the time comes?

SENDING OUT THE SEVENTY-TWO – PART 3

MULTIPLICATION

LUKE 10:1-16

During the whole time of Jesus' mission, He asked His Father, in prayer, for personal direction. And, He got it. Day in, and day out. Yet, He asked His Father for even more. He also made requests on behalf of others. His Father granted those, too. Every single time.

> **LEADERSHIP TIP #167**
>
> Have your people pray for others who will multiply your message into their worlds of influence.

Of course, the proof of prayer is always in its results. Because of the results Jesus got, His men were ready and willing to learn from Him how to pray. They could see, from the awesome things that happened, prayer was their leader's direct connection to His Father. It was His power-line.

So, when Jesus sent out the seventy-two, He instructed them to make a special request to God. "Ask Him to send more workers into the field." Jesus wanted them to pray for the multiplication factor. He knew their prayers for multiplication would be answered. Why? Because His were.

> What kind of *specific* results can you picture if you, and others in your organization, consistently prayed for God to multiply the message He has given you?

The Good Samaritan
Part One

Luke 10:29-37

One day, after the seventy-two ambassadors had reported back to Jesus, an expert in Jewish law walked up to Him. In what was, most likely, a condescending tone, he asked, "Who is my neighbor?"

Jesus could see right through the man, that he was just trying to trap

> **LEADERSHIP TIP #168**
>
> Train your people that being a good teammate means they take a personal interest in the well-being of their fellow workers.

Him. However, without hesitating, Jesus obliged. He looked into the man's eyes, and used the question to tell a short story about a Samaritan and a Jew. People from two different races who hated each other.

Jesus said that the Jewish man, on a trip, was attacked by bandits. He was robbed, stripped of his clothes, and left for dead. A Jewish priest walked up to him, took one look, and passed around him. So, did an assistant from the temple. The only person who had mercy, and did something about it, was a hated Samaritan. Jesus then asked the expert, "Which of the three was a neighbor to the man?" "The one who showed mercy," the proud lawyer quickly replied. "Yes, Jesus said, nodding approvingly, "now, go and do the same."

How can you help your people desire to help each other?

192

THE GOOD SAMARITAN

PART TWO

LUKE 10:29-37

Before we leave this episode, let's notice how Jesus got His point across to the man who was trying to trap Him. Jesus merely told a story. Okay, not just any story. He told one that would penetrate the man's smugness, and cut deep into his heart, while he still exercised his mind.

> **LEADERSHIP TIP #169**
>
> In communicating a truth to your people, tell a story that will challenge them to take action.

It's interesting that Jesus, the man who spoke with such great authority, even according to His enemies, was a storyteller. He knew how to use stories to communicate big truths. And, He would tell them with a lively and captivating style.

To be such a good storyteller, Jesus had to be a keen student of human behavior. Perhaps it was in His carpenter's shop that He learned to pay attention to detail. He also saw how different people behaved under different circumstances. Because Jesus knew people, His stories had gripping appeal. However, Jesus wasn't "just" a storyteller. He was also a great motivator. His stories normally packed a challenge for action. What's more, He expected people to take that action.

> What steps will you take to develop stories to communicate truths, that will motivate your people to take action?

MARY'S CHOICE

LUKE 10:38-42

On Jesus' last swing through the land, He and His men dipped down into the southern part. Jesus wanted to visit His old friend's in Bethany, just a short distance from Jerusalem. Of course, there were no telephones or e-mails in Jesus' day, so, people dropped by unexpectedly for visits. That

LEADERSHIP TIP #170

Make sure the busy things of life don't squeeze out your daily time at Jesus' feet.

was how Jewish people liked it. Always ready to entertain, leaving their door open for friends and strangers, alike. They felt they never knew when they might be hosting an angel from God. So, they were ready.

But, thirteen hungry men. That was something else. Talk about rushing around trying to get a meal ready. Martha was beside herself. Then, there was her sister, Mary. Instead of helping Martha, she casually sat on the floor being a sponge for every word from Jesus. Martha unraveled, and, in front of her sister, complained to Jesus about Mary not helping her. "Martha," Jesus said, gently correcting her, "there is only one thing worth being concerned about. Mary has discovered it, and I won't take it away from her."

In your busiest of times, when the pressure is on, how can you still guard your personal time with Jesus?

A HOUSE DIVIDED

LUKE 11:14-26

One day, after eating Martha's home-cooked meal, Jesus went into action. He cast a demon out of a man. People were amazed, but some of them accused Him of being able to cast out demons because He was getting His power straight from Satan.

> ## LEADERSHIP TIP #171
>
> In recruiting or hiring, select only people who will line up with your values, and whose actions match their words.

Now, that was really a stretch. You can almost see Jesus smiling and shaking His head. He must have been thinking, *What will they come up with next?* So, He told them a story. In it He equated a human body to a house. Then He connected Satan's army of demons as the residents of the house. He said Satan certainly was not going to help anyone kick his own army out of a person. That just didn't make sense. Then, He added, "A house divided against itself cannot stand."

Well, the same is true for any team, whether in the business world, in the sports world, in the military, in an organization, or, in a family. A "house" torn apart by opposing values and agendas cannot stand. It's doomed for failure, and ultimate destruction. Jesus probably was thinking, *You don't have to be a carpenter to know that.*

> What guidelines will you establish for choosing the right people?

195

DINING WITH THE ENEMY

LUKE 11:37-54

Jesus never backed down from a confrontation with the high and mighty religious leaders. One day, a Pharisee invited Him home for a meal. Now, that sounds tame enough. Yet, Jesus knew it was just a way for the Pharisee, and his cronies, to trap Him into saying something they could use in bringing a charge against Him.

LEADERSHIP TIP #172

Keep in mind that confronting an ungodly person can cause that person to come against you.

When Jesus reclined on the couch by the meal table, the host feigned "righteous" amazement that Jesus didn't ceremoniously wash His hands. After all, that was the Jewish custom. When Jesus saw His host's expression, He came right back and told the man how hypocritical he was. Then He cited several things, as a host, the Pharisee had failed to do. Of course, the host was insulted, And, when a lawyer told Jesus He was also insulted by His remarks, Jesus nailed him, too.

Talk about getting indigestion. We don't know if anyone even got a bite down. One thing we do know. The infuriated religious leaders and lawyers stepped up their efforts in trying to stop Jesus.

How will you know when it's good to carry the attack against an opponent, or to wait for a better time?

No Reason to Fear

Luke 12:4

The religious leaders were clearly elevating their attacks against Jesus. There was no longer a safe place for Him to be. Jesus' friends had to wonder how He could be so relaxed. Didn't He have a grip on reality? Well, Jesus didn't operate from this present world's viewpoint. He had an New Earth viewpoint. He lived 100% in the now. Yet, He kept His eyes fixed on the coming new world.

> **LEADERSHIP TIP #173**
>
> Help eliminate fear by knowing your physical body is but a temporary physical home you use before you receive your eternal physical home.

On that New Earth, Jesus knew He would have a different body. No longer one that was subject to cuts, bruises, tiredness, and pain. But, one, just as physical. One in which He could enjoy all the splendors of the new world, including fellowship with His Father, and every one of His followers.

Yes, Jesus had a grip on reality. That's why He taught, "Don't be afraid of those who want to kill you. They can only kill the body; they can't do any more to you." Jesus knew He would be getting a new body. In His mind, that was a fact.

> What steps will you take to keep focusing on the coming Kingdom and the different body you will have?

Every Detail of Your Life

LUKE 12:6-7

Even though the Pharisees and their cohorts were on the attack, Jesus still had thousands of people pressing around Him wherever He walked. Apparently, He wanted His disciples to realize, in the middle of all the people, how important each of them were to God. He

> **LEADERSHIP TIP #174**
>
> God knows, and is concerned about, every detail of your life.

might have even been pointing at a person with a full head of hair when He remarked, "The very hairs of your head are all numbered."

Now, in our high tech world of computers, we know the approximate number of hairs on the average person's head. A blonde, for example, has about 145,000 hairs, a dark-haired person has roughly 120,000 hairs, and a person with red hair in the neighborhood of 90,000 hairs. However, Jesus didn't teach His followers that God knew the *approximate* number. He implied God knew the *exact* number. It's no harder for God to know the number for a person with a full head of hair than it is to know for a bald person. Jesus also taught that a sparrow, which was as cheap a bird as you could buy in His day, couldn't even fall to the ground without God knowing.

> How can you communicate to the people you lead how valuable they are to God?

198

YOU'LL HAVE THE WORDS

LUKE 12:11-12

Just after Jesus told His people how valuable they were to God, He layed something heavy on them. He told them of hard times ahead. In the first century, followers of Jesus weren't guaranteed sleeping in their bed when night fell.

> **LEADERSHIP TIP #175**
>
> Boldly speak out for Jesus as you rely on the Holy Spirit to give you His words.

Satan had been using religion as a tool in trying to stop the carpenter from Nazareth. Now, Jesus predicted there would be even more religious attacks in the future, against His followers.

He said they would be brought to trial in the Jewish synagogues because of their allegiance to Him. No wandering minds among the disciples when Jesus said that. It could be a terrifying experience to speak in one's own defense. Surely, no Jewish lawyer would take their case.

Jesus knew that. So, He comforted them by promising, "Don't worry about what to say in your defense, for the Holy Spirit will teach you what needs to be said even as you are standing there."

> In what situations at work, and outside of work, might you need to become more bold in your verbal witness?

Greed Illustrated

Luke 12:13-21

As Jesus was teaching, someone from the crowd shouted out he wanted Jesus to resolve a problem he was having with his brother. It was over their inheritance. Apparently, his brother wasn't giving him his fair share. So, the brother who was drawing the shortest straw, asked Jesus to intervene.

> ## LEADERSHIP TIP #176
>
> Tell insightful stories to help people reach their own decisions, rather than make their decisions for them.

He wanted everyone's favorite teacher and mentor to set his brother straight. After all, the man figured, if Jesus told his brother to hand over his share of the inheritance to him, he would have to do so. Especially with so many witnesses.

Jesus listened, but He saw the real problem. It was greed between two brothers. Without taking sides, Jesus told a story about a farmer storing his crops in his barn. Instead of giving his surplus to the poor, the farmer decided to build a bigger barn to store all of his crops. His idea? Put away something for the future. You never know when you might need it. Jesus hit home with His point. "A person is a fool to store up earthly wealth but not have a rich relationship with God." Jesus saw this wasn't a case of mishandling wealth. It was greed.

> What helpful story can you share with one of your people who is in the middle of making a decision?

LOOKING FOR HIS RETURN

LUKE 12:35-48

The "midnight hour" for Jesus' appointment with His destiny in Jerusalem was fast approaching. He had already told His followers that, after His death, He would, at some point, return for them.

> **LEADERSHIP TIP #177**
>
> Live each moment as if it were the last, just before Jesus returns for you and the rest of His followers.

In this teaching, He made it clear He could return at anytime. No warning at all. "The Son of Man," He said, "will come at an hour you do not expect Him." Now, wasn't that a great way to keep His people on their toes? To keep them guessing.

Jesus knew if He had told His followers He was going away, and He would return in exactly two years, they wouldn't be as sharp. They wouldn't be nearly as focused each day as they would be if they thought Jesus could return at any moment.

Jesus wanted His people to be totally caught up in His agenda. So, He kept the time of His return a mystery. What does history show? Jesus' first followers lived as if He would return at any minute. Consequently, they were completely caught up in His agenda.

> What specific steps will you take to live each moment as if it were the last, just before Jesus returns?

DISCIPLINARY ACTION

LUKE 12:35-48

Jesus continued His story about servants waiting for their master's return. He told about differing degrees of punishment three of them received for not having done what their master wanted them to do.

LEADERSHIP TIP #178

When you can, discipline according to the intent of the person.

One steward was killed. Another was severely punished, and still another received only a reprimand. It seems that each punishment, or discipline, matched the degree of intent from the servant.

The first knew what his master wanted, but he was in total rebellion. He was even abusive to his fellow servants. That's the one who was killed. The severe punishment went to the second servant. He was just lazy. He didn't think his master would return so soon, so he didn't carry out the instructions.

Interestingly, even the servant who did something wrong because he didn't know any better received a light punishment. Why? Apparently to help him be more alert to what he should have been doing.

How can you determine the intent of the wrongdoer so you can match your discipline to the intent?

Families Will Be Divided

LUKE 12:49-53

Strange as it might sound, but, in this teaching, Jesus made one thing clear to His disciples. He didn't come to bring peace to this present world. The peace He spoke about would, first, be in the hearts of His followers. Then, in the coming new world. Not in this one.

LEADERSHIP TIP #179

Expect divisions among your people when Jesus becomes the issue.

In fact, it was just the opposite. Jesus warned that families would be torn apart because of Him. Those who rejected Him would even reject their own family members who had accepted Him. Siblings would turn against siblings. Children against parents, and parents against their kids. Wow. Not a pretty picture. Yet, a real one. Jesus warned that it would happen. And, as history has already confirmed Jesus' words, it has happened in millions of families.

In the 21st century, up to 95% of Americans believe in some description of God. So, the mention of "God" won't raise too many eyebrows. However, if the name "Jesus" is mentioned, it's like the person has just become a lightning rod, with the lightning about to strike.

How will you help develop harmony among your people after you do make Jesus the issue?

Understanding the Signs

LUKE 12:54-56

It must have been frustrating for Jesus to keep dealing with people who were so "tone deaf" in hearing the voice of God. Especially when the voice was coming through His own mouth.

> **LEADERSHIP TIP #180**
>
> Develop "focal points" by attaching biblical truths to natural objects and current events, to help you walk closer with God.

Most likely, Jesus paused for a moment in teaching His disciples. Hundreds of people were also pressing around Him, some even defiant to His teachings. He might well have looked upward and gazed at the sky for a few seconds. Then, He turned back to the crowd. He told them that, by looking at the sky, or feeling the south wind, they could tell whether it was going to be stormy, or sunny. Lots of heads nodded. "That's right," some of them most likely replied. Even the defiant ones had to agree.

So, why, He asked, weren't they able to interpret the current times in which they lived? He felt, if they had more accurately understood the times in which they lived, they would have been more open to what He was saying.

> 1. Select two or three natural objects, such as the sun, moon, stars, wind, trees, etc., to which you will attach a biblical truth.
>
> 2. What "focal point" will you pass on to help your people at work?

THE PATIENCE OF GOD

LUKE 13:1-9

As Jesus was talking with the people, someone reported to Him that Pilate, the Roman governor, had murdered several innocent people from Galilee. Now, it was thought, in Jesus' day, that suffering was a direct result of sin. Obviously, there is some truth to that.

LEADERSHIP TIP #181

Be patient with a person who does not accept your ideas, giving him another chance.

However, sometimes people suffer because they live in a fallen world. That was the point Jesus wanted to get across to His listeners. He wanted to help them understand the times in which they were living. So, He told a story about a man who planted a fig tree in his garden, a tree that never produced fruit. Well, the man wanted to cut the tree down. However, his servant talked him into fertilizing it, and giving it one more year to produce. The owner of the garden agreed. He could be patient with the tree for one more year.

Jesus told this story to illustrate God's patience with the people of Israel, the nation who wasn't connecting to Him and producing fruit. Yet, we can also glean from it an important principle for leadership.

When do you finally cut a person loose who just hasn't shown he is a producer?

205

Hypocrisy Check

LUKE 13:10-17

Later, on a Sabbath day, Jesus was in the synagogue teaching, when He spotted a woman with a crippling disease. He called her to come over, and He watched as she struggled to her feet.

LEADERSHIP TIP #182

Take the "Hypocrisy Check" every now and then, to make sure your actions are lined up with your values.

Totally bent over, she barely could manage to shuffle her way to the front. When she finally got there, Jesus looked down on her crippled body, and said, "Dear woman, you are healed of your disease." Then, as He reached down and touched her, she instantly straightened up. She hadn't been in that erect position for eighteen years.

Well, the leader of the synagogue was outraged. He was so caught up in religion, he couldn't see God standing in front of him. He scolded the crowd, telling them not to come and expect to be healed of anything on the Sabbath.

Jesus shot right back and called all of the officials hypocrites. "Each of you works on the Sabbath," He said. And, they did, leading their animals to water. One thing Jesus couldn't stand was the blind hypocrisy of religion.

In taking the "Hypocrisy Check, what are some things you need to work on in bringing your actions up to the standard of your values?

AN OPEN KINGDOM

LUKE 13:22-30

The Jewish people thought they were the only people who would enter the Kingdom of God. So, you can imagine, one day as Jesus was briskly walking through a village, still pressing toward Jerusalem, how shocked they were when He burst their bubble of exclusivity.

LEADERSHIP TIP #183

Plan for your work to reach out to people of all races.

Jesus said, "People will come from all over the world to take their places in the Kingdom of God." He made it clear. Real clear. Automatically becoming a citizen of God's Kingdom was not a perk for just being born a Jew. Jews also had to be born again.

That's what Jesus said to Nicodemus much earlier in His crusade. He told the famous teacher the entrance into the Kingdom was the same for everyone. No matter who they were. Jesus wasn't trying to be politically correct.

Yes, people of all races would be entering the Kingdom. From the east to the west, from the north to the south. However, each person would still have to go through the "narrow door" of Jesus Himself.

How might you need to change your mission statement to include people of all races, and how will you communicate that to your people?

Pride Before the Fall

LUKE 14:7-11

Many workers in today's world would do Charles Darwin, the father of the evolutionary theory, proud. Their code of workplace conduct is the "survival of the fittest." Each one tries to outmaneuver his own fellow workers to reach the top.

> **LEADERSHIP TIP #184**
>
> Teach your people that genuine humility is the pathway to greatness.

One day, after teaching the crowds, that's exactly what Jesus saw was happening at a banquet He was attending. He noticed how people were rushing for the better seats, the places of honor. So, Jesus, perhaps a bit amused at what was happening, passed on some advice straight from His Father.

He told the people that, by putting themselves in a place of honor, they were running the risk of embarrassment. The host could tell them to move to a different seat. Instead, it would be better to take a seat of lesser honor. Then, the host, in front of all the guests, could ask the person to take a place of greater honor. His point? It's best for other people to honor a person than for that person to honor himself.

> How can you honor your people who are genuinely humble, and who are always looking out for others, without getting them prideful of how humble they are?

THOSE WHO CAN'T REPAY

LUKE 14:12-14

At the same banquet where people were honoring themselves, Jesus saw there weren't any poor or crippled people in attendance. No lame or blind people, either. The banquet seemed to be just for the upper class people, people who had plenty of clout, and who had no apparent problems.

> **LEADERSHIP TIP #185**
>
> Train your people to give, out of a genuine concern, to those who can't repay, for God will reward their actions.

So, Jesus twisted his postion on the bench, and turned to the host. He wanted to explain how the host could really do some good with his banquets by just changing his guest list. Why just invite people who could repay him by inviting him to their house for a return meal? Why not invite people who probably wouldn't be invited anyplace else? Why not invite people who, in their wildest dreams, couldn't repay the kindness? Why not invite some of the so-called "rejects" of society?

Jesus explained that, if he will do that, "God will reward you for inviting those who could not repay you." Now, being rewarded by God isn't too shabby. Sure beats simply being invited back to one of the guest's houses.

> What program will you implement through which you can train your people to give to the people who can't repay?

THE BANQUET STORY

LUKE 14:15-24

When is a person "off duty" in helping to build God's Kingdom? When can a follower of Jesus finally relax, and not even think about it? Never, if we're using Jesus as our model.

LEADERSHIP TIP #186

Take advantage of every opportunity to tell a story that communicates one of God's truths.

At the banquet, a Jewish man was stretched out on a leather couch next to the one Jesus was on. Apparently, the man had been listening to Jesus talk to the host of the banquet. So, he turned to Jesus and mentioned it would be a great blessing to attend a banquet in the Kingdom of God. Jesus could have just nodded politely, and kept on eating. Instead, He stopped eating, faced the man, and replied with a story.

It was of a man who had invited many people to his banquet. However, each person came up with an excuse why he couldn't attend. So, the man sent his servant out into the streets to invite everyone who seemed to be on the downside of life. The point was clear to the Jewish man, and he probably nodded in agreement. God's Kingdom was definitely not the future home for Jews only. It was open for everyone.

What stories can you tell about the truths of God that are most important to you, stories that can inspire others?

TOTAL COMMITMENT

LUKE 14:25-26

After the banquet, Jesus took to the street, with a large crowd following after Him. As He glanced over His shoulder, He knew the people wanted to learn more. So, turning around, and perhaps walking backward a few steps as He spoke, He gave them quite an attention-grabbing challenge.

LEADERSHIP TIP #187

Select for the highest level of training only those who can give you their total commitment.

"If you want to be my disciple," He said, "you must hate everyone else -- your father and mother, wife and children, brothers and sisters -- yes, even your own life. Otherwise, you cannot be my disciple."

Whoa, what did He mean by "hate every one else?" True, God wants all family members to love one another. He has made that clear all the way through the Bible. Yet, compared to the love Jesus' followers needed to have for Him, He wanted their love for a family member to look almost as if it were a hatred. The word He used was one of comparison. Okay, you won't get that same level of love from your people. But, you do need to ask for a great commitment from anyone you want to take to the highest level of training.

What level of loyalty will you require for the highest level of training, and how will you communicate it to your people?

211

COUNTING THE COST

PART ONE

LUKE 14:27-32

Today, many of Jesus' followers introduce others to Him using a "sales" approach. Just pray this quick prayer, and He will be in your life. It's quick, easy, and painless. And, everyday will be better than the day before. They give the impression that becoming a follower will take less time than buy-

> **LEADERSHIP TIP #188**
>
> Have a person consider the cost before making a commitment to follow Jesus.

ing a hamburger, and with less commitment.

Jesus used a different approach. First, He described the commitment He was looking for. "If you do not carry your own cross and follow me," He said, "you cannot be my disciple." He was saying, unless a person was willing to die for his commitment to Him, he couldn't be a follower. Then, He said a person, before making that commitment, should consider the cost. He told about how a builder would first calculate whether, or not, he had enough money to complete the project. Before he started it, that is. That's the kind of calculating the cost Jesus wanted all of His followers to do.

1. Why does a person need to consider the cost of following Jesus?

2. How can you help a person consider the cost of being a follower?

COUNTING THE COST

PART TWO

LUKE 14:27-32

My friend, a former CFO of Silver Dollar City in Branson, Missouri, one of the world's finest theme parks, told me of a situation he was put in when he was just breaking into the corporate world in Texas.

His boss gave him two major projects to work

> **LEADERSHIP TIP 189**
>
> Have your people consider what it will take to accomplish a task before telling you they will do it.

on, both having a completion date in the same time frame. My friend calculated the time it would take for each project. He concluded he couldn't give either of the projects his best effort. So, he went to his boss, and "put the ball in his boss's court." He explained what each project would take. Then, he asked his boss to make the decision. Did his boss want him to give a 100% effort doing just one project, or give a mediocre effort on both of them? His boss accepted the "ball," and told him to just focus on one of the projects.

Good thinking on the bosses part, and really good thinking on my friend's part. It mirrored the challenge Jesus gave those following after Him, to calculate the cost.

> What guidelines will you give your people to help them consider the cost for each project, and assignment?

Giving Up Ownership

Luke 14:33

Jesus told the people, following Him along the dirt road, "You cannot become My disciple without giving up everything you own." Now, let's not mis-understand what He was saying.

Jesus was not telling them to get rid of all their possessions, and then ask other people to support them as they committed themselves to follow Him. That would be counter-productive. If everyone ended up following Jesus, and that is His desire, who would support His followers? Everyone would be one.

> **LEADERSHIP TIP #190**
>
> Mentally turn over the ownership of all your possessions to God, and live as His manager of them in building His Kingdom.

Here's what Jesus was really challenging the people to do. He was talking about giving up the *ownership* of their posses-sions. When people commit themselves to become one of His followers, they're turning the ownership of their possessions over to God. So, instead of "owning" their possessions, they are simply God's "manager" of them. That means each fol-lower of Jesus must ask God what He wants them to do with their resources. And, then, do it.

> Consider writing a document in which you turn over the ownership of your possessions to God, and sign on as His manager.

The Open Arms Policy

Luke 15:1-10

The "outcasts" of the land loved hearing Jesus teach. And, He welcomed them with open arms. Jesus was just as much at home with the very shady characters as He was with His followers. Of course, the religious authorities criticized Him for mixing with such "sinners." So, one day when the au-

> **LEADERSHIP TIP #191**
>
> Develop a way to use your "organization" to introduce people, of every walk of life, to Jesus.

thorities came to Him with their criticism, Jesus told them two stories. Each one illustrated His purpose of recruiting "lost" people into God's forever family.

First, Jesus told about a man who owned a hundred sheep. One day, one of his sheep strayed off from the rest. The owner couldn't take a break until he searched high and low, and finally found the critter. Then, Jesus told about a woman who had ten silver coins. However, one of the coins dropped off the table and rolled into a crevice. The woman couldn't stop looking until she found the lost coin. Both the shepherd and the woman celebrated after finding what they were after.

1. What opportunities do you and your people have in mixing with people outside of God's Kingdom?

2. How will you help introduce those people to Jesus?

The Wayward Son

LUKE 15:11-32

Next, Jesus told the religious upper hierarchy a story about the son of a wealthy man. The son went to his dad, one day, and demanded his future inheritance. He wanted it while he was still young enough to enjoy all the pleasures of the world the money could buy.

> **LEADERSHIP TIP #192**
>
> Welcome back into fellowship any Christian who genuinely repents after being out of fellowship with Jesus.

The father thought about it. Then, he wisely, gave his son the freedom to make an unwise choice. The son did, and the father went along with it.

In a short time, the son had wasted his inheritance on quick pleasures. He ended up whipped by the world, and groveling for food in a pigpen. That's when he came to his senses. Suddenly, life back home didn't look so bad, after all. After running through his mind, several times, how he would approach his father, the son went home. He was a shadow of his former self. The father, who had been looking for the return of his son, raced out and warmly embraced him. No chiding, no sarcasm, and no "I told you so." Just lots of celebrating.

> How might God want you to be His conduit for welcoming a repentant Christian back into fellowship, and how would you know if he really was repentant?

216

THE WAYWARD STAFF

LUKE 15:11-32

Now, let's see how Jesus' story about the wayward son, and the forgiving father, applies to you and your particular team of people. Not everyone, all the time, will be marching to the vision you've given your people. Or, to how you want them to "march." Violations will occur both in actions and in attitudes. So, how do you deal with them?

LEADERSHIP TIP #193

Welcome back into good standing any of your people who sincerely ask your forgiveness for a wrongdoing, and who has complied with your regulations that affect his behavior.

First, be true to the disciplinary action you've established in your manual. Don't make an exception just because the disciplinary action might jeopardize a project. That would send a signal that would be far more dangerous than choking the project.

Second, in taking Jesus' story to heart, do exactly what the father in the story did. Welcome back into fellowship a repentant staff. The purpose of Jesus' stories was always to communicate truths straight from God. And, remember this. You are God's conduit to the people He has assigned you to lead.

How is your carrying out disciplinary action, as well as welcoming the person back, similar to what happened in Jesus' story?

Dealing With Jealousy

LUKE 15:25-32

In Jesus' story, the father decided to throw a banquet to celebrate the return of his wayward son. Well, the fatted calf wasn't the only critter unhappy about the father's decision. The older brother wasn't too crazy about it, either.

In fact, the green-eyed monster of jealousy took

LEADERSHIP TIP #194

Help neutralize one of your people's jealousy for your attention by explaining, and showing, how you really do care for him.

a strangle hold on him. As the band played celebratory music in the background, the only thing the older son could think about was all the years he had put in for his father. What did he ever get in return? Certainly no banquet in his honor.

In Jesus' story, the older son rushed up to his father and complained. However, the wise father helped his son get perspective. He explained that, for the many years of loyalty his older son had given him, he was getting something far better than a banquet. He was getting the entire estate. Not really a bad exchange. For the son, that is.

1. By what the older son told his father, what can you determine about his attitude in working for his father?

2. How can you determine if a complaint you hear has jealously at its roots?

The Creative Steward

LUKE 16:1-12

Walking along, Jesus now turned His attention to His twelve man team. He had a story for them. It was about an estate manager who had been wasting his employer's money. When the boss got wind of it, he told his manager to get ready to make a report. After the report, he would be fired.

> **LEADERSHIP TIP #195**
>
> Creatively, use your resources to help others in a way that pleases God, and train your people to do the same. You will be rewarded.

So, the manager, very shrewdly, invited some of his friends, who he knew owed his boss money, to come in and he would settle their accounts. Still acting in his role as manager, he cut everyone's debt. Obviously, those people were grateful, and they owed the manager big time. Even his boss had to admit the manager finally showed some spunk, some creativity.

Well, Jesus' men must have been scratching their collective heads. Was their mentor actually telling them to be dishonest? No, Jesus was quick to point out. "Here's the lesson," He said. "Use your worldly resources to benefit others and make friends. Then, when your earthly possessions are gone, they will welcome you to an eternal home."

> How can you have pure motives in using your resources for others when Jesus said you, most likely, would benefit from your kindness?

The Rich Man and Lazarus

LUKE 16:19-31

Next, Jesus turned back to the Pharisees in the crowd. He could see they were still "chomping at the bit" to take Him down. So, He told them a story about a man named Lazarus.

LEADERSHIP TIP #196

Look for opportunities to use your resources to help the poor in your community, and give a vision for your people to do the same.

Strangely, the Lazarus in His story, is the only person in all of the stories Jesus told who had a name. This has led some Bible scholars to conclude Jesus was telling a story about a real happening. Well, regardless of whether it was real, or not, the truths in the parable are clear.

First, the world is filled with the wealthy who pay no attention to the poor. Second, there really is a future life after this present one is over. Third, people who have died, and are in the place of torment, will still have a memory of what happened in their lifetime. And, because of that memory, they will be filled with regrets. Finally, and for some unexplainable reason, even if some people know a person has returned from the dead, they wouldn't accept what they said about God and His ways. Jesus' message? Don't be like the rich man.

How can caring for people who are unable to care for themselves be honoring to God?

No Thanks Expected

LUKE 17:7-10

After telling the Pharisees the story about the rich man and Lazarus, Jesus decided to teach His men a valuable lesson. He likened the life of service to which He was calling His men to the life of a lowly servant in their day. Now, a servant was expected to do whatever his master told him to do. No back talk. No argu-

> **LEADERSHIP TIP #197**
>
> Teach your people to give their best in serving, as though they were doing it for God Himself, without any regard for thanks or recognition from others.

ing. And, no trying to get only lighter duties. Perhaps, with a smile, Jesus asked, "Does the master thank the servant for doing what he was told to do?" Then, with an emphatic shake of His head, "Of course not."

His point? A servant serves without the need for a "thank you." The code by which servants lived was simply to do what they were told to do…period. That code was the message onto which Jesus wanted His followers to grab. Sure, it was only natural for His men to expect someone to thank them for a service. Yet, Jesus taught His followers to serve others, without expecting any thanks. He wanted them to know their thanks would come from God. He is a good giver of thanks.

> At the same time you are showing gratitude for your people, how can you train them to serve others without expecting gratitude?

The Bond of Misfortune

LUKE 17:11-19

Jews and Samaritans, all living in the same, small land, hated each other like cats and dogs. One day, as Jesus walked up to the border of Galilee and Samaria, a group of lepers, mostly Jews with at least one Samaritan, crossed paths with Him.

> **LEADERSHIP TIP #198**
>
> As you observe your people, keep in mind that a shared experience of misfortune can help break down barriers of hostility.

Because leprosy was considered unclean and highly contagious, a leper's friends and family members would often disown him. Some families even considered a leper to be dead. To top it off, lepers had to shout, "Unclean...unclean," whenever they were near other people. It was a warning to keep people the safe, six-foot distance from them.

Sometimes, if the wind was blowing, their putrid smell of rotting flesh would alert people. Even before they heard the warning. Interestingly, lepers didn't see each other as different races. With lepers, the wall of hostility between Jews and Samaritans was broken down.

They were simply lepers.

> What are ways that a shared experience of misfortune can bring people together? And, how can they maintain harmony after the experience is past?

Only a Samaritan returns

Luke 17:11-19

To honor Jesus, the ten lepers kept their distance. They just called out for Him to have mercy on them. Apparently, they saw in Jesus their last ray of hope to be cleansed of a disease that was eating up their bodies.

LEADERSHIP TIP #199

Model to your people the "art" of showing gratitude to those who help you.

Their skin might have already been decaying, and their nerve ends already deadened. Some of them might even have had their eyes crusted over.

Jesus, in a show of compassion, yelled back for them to go and show themselves to the priests. Now, wait a minute. That was something a person did who had already been cleansed of leprosy. Not someone who still had the disease. The priest would then confirm the cleansing.

However, in obedience, the ten lepers started down the road to find a priest. Amazingly, as they took their first few steps, God totally cleansed each of them. Only one returned to thank the carpenter from Nazareth. Only the Samaritan.

He returned to thank a Jew.

Jesus already taught that a servant didn't need to be thanked. So, why did He make an issue about only one of the ten returning to thank Him?

Determined Prayer

LUKE 18:1-8

Jesus knew that, after His mission on earth was finished, His followers would need to rely heavily on the same incredible tool He used to stay connected to God.

Prayer.

However, Jesus wanted His disciples to know that God doesn't always grant

LEADERSHIP TIP #200

Keep in mind that God will give what is best for you as you persistently pray.

requests within the first ten minutes. He didn't want them to lose heart and give up in their praying if they didn't see results right away. So, Jesus told His followers a story about one very determined lady. She was a widow.

Apparently, someone in town was out to take what was rightfully hers. She took the matter to a heartless judge, hoping for justice. Not caring much about people, the judge refused to help her. But she kept at him…and, at him…and, at him. Finally, he gave in, just to get her off his back.

Now, why did Jesus tell that story? That "keep-at-it" approach the woman used was the same approach Jesus wanted His followers to have in prayer. The same approach He used.

If God is going to grant your Christlike request, why doesn't He always do it right away?

TWO MEN PRAYING

LUKE 18:9-14

Pharisees were noted for their public prayers. Yet, in listening to them, Jesus could see they were really praying for show, not praying to God. One of the things Jesus couldn't stand in the Pharisees was their superficiality with God. Especially in their prayers. They came to God almost on a high-

LEADERSHIP TIP #201

Give honor to your people who deserve it, but who don't call attention to themselves.

er level than He was on. So, to help His followers understand the importance of humility, Jesus told them a story about two men praying in the temple.

One, a Pharisee, prayed out loud. He was hoping to call attention to what a wonderful person he was. The other, a hated tax-collector, unassumingly came before God. He owned up that he was a sinner. He simply cried out for God to be forgiving, not claiming at all that he was deserving. The sobering statement Jesus left for His followers to ponder was: "For everyone who exalts himself will be humbled, and he who humbles himself will be exalted." He wanted each of His men to figure out what that meant for themselves.

1. Why is humility so important from God's viewpoint?

2. What honor can you give a person that won't cause him to be less humble?

225

THE COMPARISON TRAP

LUKE 18:9-14

Jesus knew how subtle the "comparison trap" worked on people. He didn't want his followers to be trapped by it. So, in the same story He was telling about the two men praying, He used the arrogant Pharisee to paint a word picture.

> **LEADERSHIP TIP #202**
>
> Compare yourself only to the standard Jesus modeled, not to that of any other person.

He wanted to show how comparing with other people misses the mark of God's best. The Pharisee, in the story, said, "I thank you I'm not like other men..." His idea was, "Hey, compared to those people, I'm really good."

Well, Mr. Pharisee, how are you compared to Jesus? That was the point Jesus wanted to get across to His men. He didn't want them to compare themselves to other people. They could always find someone they could outshine. How are they doing compared to the standard Jesus set for them? That was the real, bottom-line question. If they were going to compare themselves with someone else, let it be Jesus Himself.

1. How can comparing yourself with other people keep you from being the best God has designed you to be?

2. What standard can you set for your people that will draw the best out of them all the time?

Heterosexual Marriages

MATTHEW 19:3-6

Before Jesus had even started out on His mission, Satan tried to derail Him in the wilderness. Satan, of course, failed, but he didn't give up. During the years Jesus walked the roads of Palestine, Satan kept up his attack on Him, mainly through the religious establishment. One day, as Jesus and His entourage walked into

> **LEADERSHIP TIP #203**
>
> In your work, honor families with perks, only if the marriages are between male and female.

Judea, just east of the Jordan River, a few scheming Pharisees approached Him. They had a question they thought might entrap Him. "Is it lawful," one of them asked, "for a man to divorce his wife for any reason at all?"

Jesus answered by giving His enemies a quick lesson in genetics. He told them that, from the beginning, God made male and female. Then, He brought His answer home by saying that, once a *male* and *female* are united in marriage, only unfaithfulness is grounds for divorce. Now, as you read this passage, don't go too fast over the gender terms, male and female.

1. How can you justify honoring only heterosexual marriages, and not same-sex marriages?

2. Why does God only honor marriages between male and female?

227

ONLY GROUNDS FOR DIVORCE

MATTHEW 19:7-12

The Pharisees were always looking for loop-holes in God's standard. However, in the divorce issue, they didn't think they had to look for a loop-hole. Moses had already given them one. At least, that's how the Pharisees read Scripture. So, in their attempt to entrap the carpenter with His

LEADERSHIP TIP #204

Give your people training in developing a God-honoring marriage.

own words, in front of all the people, they asked Jesus about Moses granting divorces with just a certificate. They wanted to know how Jesus got off saying that adultery -- sex outside of marriage -- was the only legitimate grounds for divorce.

The desperate religious leaders thought they had finally corralled Jesus. Here they found Him in direct opposition to Moses, the great leader of the Jewish nation. In Jesus' reply, He actually set His teaching up as a higher standard than what Moses gave. Not a very diplomatic approach. But, then again, Jesus wasn't trying to make friends within the religious establishment. He just wanted to give the truth, straight from God.

1. What can you put in your guidelines that will explain God's standard for marriage, and why might it be important for you to do so?

2. How will you develop a marriage enrichment training program for your people?

228

Twelve Hours of Daylight

John 11:1-9

Jesus didn't just model everything He taught. He also explained it in ways people could understand. Another object lesson was coming up. As Jesus and His followers were walking the roads of the land, still some distance from Jerusalem, one of Jesus' good friends, Lazarus, was

> **LEADERSHIP TIP #205**
>
> Rely on God to protect and enable you to do the work He has called you to do.

deathly ill. His two sisters, Mary and Martha, sent word to Jesus about him. However, instead of rushing to Lazarus' side to heal him, Jesus hung back for another couple of days. Not something you would expect from a caring friend. Unless, of course, the caring friend had something greater in mind.

After two days, Jesus told His men He was going to Lazarus. That caught them off guard. They tried to convince Him not to go, that it would be too dangerous in the Jerusalem area. The temple religious leaders were out to get Him. Jesus countered by asking, "Are there not twelve hours in the day? A man who walks by day will not stumble…" Now, what did Jesus mean? One line of thought is: If you walk in the light of God's leading, He will protect you.

> How can you interpret this application in view of even missionaries being killed as they pursue God's assignment for them?

229

A BOLD CLAIM

JOHN 11:17-27

Because of the warm climate and no embalming of the dead, when a Jewish person died, the body was put into a tomb very quickly. So, when Jesus arrived on the outskirts of Bethany, Lazarus had already been buried in the side of a cave for four days. Lazarus must have been a man of some wealth. At least, of some

> **LEADERSHIP TIP #206**
>
> Keep an eternal viewpoint as you participate in your activities. Ask, "What impact will this have on eternity?"

influence. Those are the people who got the caves. The poorer people were simply buried in the ground.

Neighbors and people from the surrounding area walked over to Mary and Martha's house. While they were consoling the two sisters, Martha received word that Jesus was nearby. She quickly left the house, and hurried out to Him. Full of grief, she told Jesus, "If only you had been here, my brother would not have died." She probably was wondering why Jesus hadn't come sooner. The two had a brief conversation about life after death. Then, Jesus looked into her eyes and said, "I am the resurrection and the life. He who believes in me will live, even though he dies; and whoever lives and believes in me will never die. Do you believe this?"

What does Jesus' comment to Martha mean, and what does it imply?

EMPATHY IN ACTION

JOHN 11:17-35

Martha returned to the house, and whispered to her sister that Jesus wanted to see her. He was waiting outside the village. Most likely, Jesus didn't want get any closer to the house. People would have rushed up to Him, and forgot why they were there.

LEADERSHIP TIP #207

Use logic to communicate with someone who is being logical, and use compassionate understanding to communicate with someone who is being emotional.

When the neighbors saw Mary leave so fast, they figured she was going out to the tomb. So, they followed along. She ran all the way to Jesus, wiping tears from her face with every other stride. She was an emotional wreck. Interestingly, Mary actually said the same thing to Jesus as her sister did. Only it took longer because she was crying so hard. "Lord…sob, sob…if you had been here…sob, sob, sob…my brother…sob…would not have died…oh…boo hoo."

Jesus looked at her and simply asked where her brother was buried. Tears started trickling down His cheeks, too. With Martha, Jesus was logical because Martha was logical. With Mary, Jesus was emotional because Mary was emotional.

1. Why doesn't logic communicate with emotion?

2. How will you train your people to use this application?

A DEAD MAN LIVES

JOHN 11:36-44

A Palestinian tomb in a cave had an opening, but no door at the entrance. At the opening, however, men would dig a ditch. Then, a huge boulder, the shape of an ox-cart wheel, weighing about 2000 pounds, was rolled against the open area. The depth of the ditch held the boulder in place as it leaned flush against the wall, covering the entrance.

LEADERSHIP TIP #208

God will help you overcome what appears to be insurmountable odds, if it is His plan for you to do so.

When Jesus and His entourage approached the tomb, He told some of the men to roll back the boulder. Martha quickly spoke up, "But Lord, by this time there's a bad odor." Apparently, Martha thought Jesus had just wanted to have one last look at His friend's face. She didn't think a decomposing body would be the right thing to view. To say nothing of the stench.

However, Jesus insisted, and the men rolled back the boulder. Then, after openly praying, Jesus looked directly into the dark tomb, and called, "Lazarus, come out." Onlookers gasped as the linen-bound Lazarus, very much alive, hopped his way to the entrance. Against all the odds.

How might Jesus bringing Lazarus back to life apply to a difficult challenge you're facing?

PRIORITIES

MARK 10:17-22

Lazarus was out of the tomb, and Jesus had left the Jerusalem area. It wasn't quite His time. As He and His men were walking along a dirt road, a rich man ran up and fell down on his knees before Him. The man had a question burning inside of him.

> **LEADERSHIP TIP #209**
>
> Let go of anything that doesn't come under the "umbrella" of what God has called you to do.

"What do I need to do to have eternal life?" he asked. Apparently the man had all he wanted of material possessions. He was at a point in which he was thinking about life after the current one was over. To his credit, with all of his wealth, he thought there had to be something more.

However, Jesus looked into the man's very nature. He could see the man really loved his material possessions. He didn't just think of himself as a steward of them. He owned them. More to the point, they owned him. So, Jesus hit him where he needed to be hit. "Go, sell what you have," Jesus told him, eager for the man's response, "and give it all to the poor." The man, slowly rose to his feet. Totally disappointed, he turned and walked away. Jesus was disappointed, too.

1. Why did Jesus tell the man to give it all to the poor?

2. How might you be putting other things ahead of God's plan for you?

Getting Into Heaven

MARK 10:23-27

Jesus knew that people normally thought of getting into Heaven as a reward for how good they have been in their present life. He didn't want His team to fall into that wrong way of thinking.

LEADERSHIP TIP #210

Material resources are a gift from God to use for His purposes through you. Rely on God to show you how He wants you to use them.

So, as the rich man sadly walked away, Jesus chose to get across a truth to His men. He said that not even a rich person could have life with God in the new world by his own merit.

To illustrate what He meant, He said, "In fact, it is easier for a camel to go through the eye of a needle than for a rich person to enter the Kingdom of God!" Now, let's focus on just two points. First, Jesus was referring to a real camel, and an actual sewing needle. Not an archway, sometimes called the "eye of a needle." Jesus was showing the impossibility of anyone "buying" their way into God's forever Kingdom. Second, the carpenter from Nazareth was not against wealth. He was against how some people used their wealth. Just for themselves. Not the way God wanted them to use it.

How can you know for sure how God wants you to use the material resources He has brought your way?

FAMILY BENEFITS

MARK 10:28-31

As Jesus told about the camel and the eye of a needle, Peter was mentally calculating, probably wondering, *What am I going to get out of my loyalty? After all, I could have had quite a fishing fleet by now, if I would have just focused on that.*

> **LEADERSHIP TIP #211**
>
> As a member of God's family, you have many resources available to you in this present world, and in your forever life in the next.

"We've given up everything to follow you," Peter said. Then, with His usual deep, penetrating insight, Jesus answered all of Peter's questions. He said anyone who left everything to follow Him would get it back at least a hundredfold in this present life, as well as in the life to come.

Okay, how does the "hundredfold" happen in this life when it's obvious many committed followers don't experience that? When a person becomes a follower of Jesus, he immediately becomes a member of a vast family. Ideally, if Christians treated each other as family, a "new world" of benefits would open to each one. Jesus also said, His followers would be persecuted in this present world. Jesus always spoke the truth. What He said about the "hundredfold" was the truth.

> What can you do through your work and church to help Christians experience what Jesus promised?

235

Last Becomes First

Matthew 20:1-16

In the Palestine of Jesus' day, owners of vineyards would go to the marketplace early in the morning to hire workers for harvesting. Jesus picked up on that routine. He wanted to teach His followers how life in the world to come was an act of God's unmerited love, not His deserved justice.

LEADERSHIP TIP #212

Keep in mind that life in God's Kingdom is a gift from God, not a vacation you have purchased with your good works.

In Jesus' story, the owner of a vineyard agreed to pay a group of workers one denarius, a Roman silver coin, for 12 hours of work. That was the daily wage for a worker. Later, at different times of the day, including the 11th hour, the owner promised new groups of workers the same wage. Exactly the same wage.

Now, the first group of workers complained that the workers hired at the 11th hour were getting just as much as they were, for only one hour of work. The owner replied that it was his right to pay whatever he chose. Everyone he hired agreed to the wage. How the owner chose to spend his money was up to him. No one else.

What does it mean to you that eternal life in God's coming new world is a gift from Him out of His love for you, rather than something you have earned, based on your own goodness?

Keep Your Word

Matthew 20:1-16

In Jesus' story about the workers in the vineyard, He wanted His listeners to grab hold of God's love. Life in the Forever Kingdom had nothing to do with one's own good works.

LEADERSHIP TIP #213

Be faithful to your agreement with others, regardless of what other people receive.

Now, let's camp on the main problem of the first group of workers. Jesus carefully wove into His story how those first workers compared themselves to the last workers hired. The first group had done most of the work, so they figured they should be paid more. Ah, the "comparison trap" strikes again.

The idea the owner wanted to get across is the first group of workers was paid exactly what they agreed to accept. The owner thought they ought to live by the agreed-upon terms. They shouldn't expect something more simply because someone else got the same for lesser work.

A side point that Jesus seemed to want to get across was that His followers should be true to their word, and not fall into the "comparison trap."

1. Why does God want you to keep your word?

2. How can you diplomatically help your people avoid comparing themselves with others?

A CANDID WARNING

MARK 10:32-34

For Jesus, it was a lonely road to Jerusalem. As He was walking a few steps ahead of His men, perhaps thinking about what would really happen to Him on the cross, His men were terrified.

LEADERSHIP TIP #214

Candidly, warn your people about future dangers, so they can turn back, if they choose.

They knew Jerusalem would be a hot spot for Jesus. Consequently, it would be for them, too. The disciples knew the religious leaders had, lately, become more aggressive. They feared for their good friend's life. For their own, as well.

Jesus sensed their uneasiness and fear. So, He stopped, turned around, perhaps wiped some sweat from His face, and called His men in for a little "pep talk." Jesus described to them what would happen to the Son of Man, down to the detail. He said, "They will mock Him, spit on Him, flog him with a whip, and kill Him, but after three days He will rise again."

Those last four words were the "pep" of Jesus' talk. Yet, at that time, His men could only think about their friend's agonizing death. And, the uncertainty of what would happen to them.

Why would you take the risk in having your people leave you after you tell them of the dangers ahead?

A Selfish Request

MARK 10:35-45

On the road to Jerusalem, strife broke out in camp. Two of Jesus' men daringly asked Him if they could be given His most trusted positions when He set up God's Kingdom on earth. They were ready to accept greater responsibility in the coming Kingdom, as long as they got recognized for it. Jesus asked them if they could handle being swallowed up in the suffering He would have to undergo. They, brashly, said they could do it.

> **LEADERSHIP TIP #215**
>
> Model for your people that true leadership is in serving others.

Jesus had to smile a bit. Their words showed their complete lack of understanding. The two brothers had no idea how bad it was going to get. Unfortunately, they failed to get out of ear shot of the other disciples when they asked Jesus. So when the ten overheard the request, they were furious. It was like the two brothers had beaten them to the request. In the middle of the squabbling, Jesus decided it was time for a team meeting. He called His men over, and probably had them sit down on the ground beside Him. Then, He put it in plain words. "Whoever wants to be a leader among you must be your servant, and whoever wants to be first among you must be the slave of everyone else." They got His point. At least, for the moment.

> How will you model the servant-leader role to your people?

HEALING OF A BLIND MAN

LUKE 18:35-43

On the road, Jesus and His men were walking into Jericho, a town about 18 miles from Jerusalem. A blind beggar was sitting on the roadside with a few other people when Jesus and His large crowd walked by. Other people were lining the road just to get a glimpse

LEADERSHIP TIP #216

Remember, as you bring your requests to God, He likes persistence.

of the famous leader. When the blind man asked who it was who passed him, one of the bystanders told him it was Jesus.

Flashing through the man's mind must have been all the reports he had heard from travelers about the different people Jesus had healed. Spontaneously, the blind man braced himself and stood up. He screamed out for Jesus to have mercy on him. People lining the road tried to shut the man up, but he just got louder. And, more determined.

Jesus finally heard the man's voice crying out. He stopped in His tracks, turned around and spotted him. He then asked someone to bring the man to Him. Soon, the blind man was standing in front of Jesus, hearing Him ask, "What do you want me to do for you?" Without hesitation, the man blurted out, "Lord, I want to see." In that same brief moment, Jesus restored the man's sight. Faster than the twinking of an eye.

What can we learn about Jesus from this episode?

240

An Ear to the People

LUKE 18:35-43

Let's recapture the scene. As Jesus walked by the blind man, He was totally caught up in teaching. People were pressing all around Him, even bumping into each other. Now, here is what's interesting.

LEADERSHIP TIP #217

God definitely hears you when you bring your special needs to Him.

As much as Jesus was riveted on what He was teaching, He picked up on the crying out of the blind man. He heard his plea for help, and He turned around to find the man in the crowd.

Okay, why is that so important? Remember, Jesus is the visible expression of our invisible God (John 1:18). What Jesus did is what God does. What Jesus said, is what God wants us to know. When Jesus is alert to a person's needs, God is alert to a person's needs.

The point is that Jesus did not see the blind man as an interruption to what He was doing. In fact, He sent one of the people following after Him to bring the blind man to Him. The blind man became Jesus' top priority for that moment.

1. How can God hear each request coming to Him at the same time He is listening to millions of other people talking to Him?

2. What does Jesus' attentiveness mean to you?

241

Time With Zacchaeus

LUKE 19:1-10

Jericho was a rich town, and it was a link between Jerusalem and the lands to the east. In fact, Josephus, the famous Jewish historian called it a "divine region."

LEADERSHIP TIP #218

Train your people to be genuinely friendly to all people, even the "rejects" of society. God can use those encounters to change people.

Now, there was living in that rich town a wealthy tax-collector, by the name of Zacchaeus. The rascal had built up his fortune by overcharging people. In other words, ripping them off.

Zacchaeus had heard Jesus was entering town. He, like everyone else, was curious about Him. So, he raced along the road trying to catch a glimpse of the famous teacher. However, Zacchaeus had a problem. He was so short he couldn't see over the heads of the crowds already lining the street to see Jesus walk by. Being a quick thinker, Zacchaeus raced down the road, found a Sycamore tree, climbed it, and waited.

He almost fell out of the tree, in shock. Jesus stopped, looked up and said, "Zacchaeus, come down. I must be a guest in your house today." Having a close-up visit with Jesus for those few hours totally transformed the corrupt tax-collector.

How can you train your people to be genuinely friendly to all the people God puts in their paths?

THE TEN SERVANTS

LUKE 19:11-27

After spending the night with Zacchaeus, Jesus took to the streets of Jericho for more teaching. Walking along, He told the crowd a story, partly based on a real incident. When Herod the Great died, his kingdom was divided among his three sons. The splitting up, however, had to be con-

> **LEADERSHIP TIP #219**
>
> Use ALL the resources God has given you to bring an increase to His Kingdom. He will reward you.

firmed by the Roman emperor. So, each of Herod's three sons had to travel to Rome to be confirmed, or approved, as king.

In Jesus' story, a nobleman went away to be approved. Before he left, he gave ten servants different amounts of money. He wanted them to invest it while he was gone. When he returned, the newly approved king called his servants in for an accounting. The first two servants reported profit earnings of ten and five times the amount of money they were given to invest. To each, the king rewarded them with the same number of cities to rule over as the profit they showed. However, when the third servant reported no profit, the king was furious. He took what that servant had, and divided it among the others who made a profit. Jesus then said, "To those who use well what they are given, even more will be given."

> What specific resources do you have that you need to invest for God?

243

Rewards From God

Luke 19:11-27

Jesus knew that people, no matter how great their cause, can get tired. Some, even to the point of burning out, by continually giving of themselves. In this story, Jesus wanted His followers to get a glimpse of how His Father was going to reward them for the work they did for Him in this world.

LEADERSHIP TIP #220

God will reward you in the world to come for the work you've done for Him in this world.

Jesus wanted them to engrave that glimpse on their minds.

Why? So, when they started to drag a bit, they might get a recharge? How? By thinking about the bona-fide reward that would someday be theirs.

Did you notice the nobleman rewarded his first two servants based on the profit they showed? In their new kingdom, these two servants were given authority in direct proportion to what they did in the old kingdom, before the nobleman actually returned as king. That's the picture of reality Jesus wanted His followers to have about their work in this present world. It will continue on in the next. People will have work that's best suited to their abilities. It will be a perfect match.

1. What work do you see yourself doing in the coming new world?

2. How can you improve your work for the Lord?

Increasing Responsibility

Luke 19:11-27

Like in most of Jesus' stories, there's more than one connection to the reality of life. We've already seen how God will reward followers of Jesus for their work for Him in this world.

> **LEADERSHIP TIP #221**
>
> Give your people increased authority and responsibility based on the quality of their present work.

Now, let's see the connection of that same story to you and the people you lead. In John 1:18, we learn that Jesus was the visible expression, or "snapshot" of our invisible God. So, what we learn directly from Jesus is what we're learning directly from God.

In 2 Corinthians 5:20, we also learn that Jesus' followers are His personal ambassadors, or representatives, in this world. Consequently, what we learn from Jesus is also something He wants us to carry out in our own work. That includes the giving out of rewards to the people we lead for tasks well done. The reward Jesus is going to give is increased authority and responsibility. That's a good model for rewards today, too.

1. What added authority and responsibility can you use to reward your people?

2. How will you know when to reward your people?

Giving the Best

John 12:1-8

Mary, her brother, Lazarus, and her sister, Martha, all lived together in the village of Bethany, just on the outskirts of Jerusalem. Lazarus was the man Jesus returned to life, so people naturally milled around their house, all trying to get a glimpse of the man who once was dead. Lazarus had become an instant regional celebrity.

> **LEADERSHIP TIP #222**
>
> Give the best quality of what you have as a token of your love for Jesus.

However, when Jesus and His followers were spotted walking toward their friend's house, people quickly spread the word. Crowds, just as quickly, overflowed the area. Everyone wanted to see Jesus. Then, after Jesus and His men ate the meal Martha prepared for them, with people looking in from outside, Mary did something unusual. As Jesus was stretching out on a bench, she broke open a jar of expensive perfume, knelt down by His feet and rubbed the perfume on them. After that, letting her hair loose, she used her flowing hair to dry His feet. Similar to what a woman earlier had done.

> 1. Describe what you can do on a current project to express the quality of your love for Jesus.
>
> 2. How can you train your people to express the quality of their love for God in their work?

Finding a Donkey

LUKE 19:28-35

While resting in Bethany, knowing His death wasn't far away, Jesus told two of His disciples to go into another village and lead back a donkey. He wanted to ride the animal into Jerusalem.

Notice how specific He was in His instructions. 1) Go into the village. 2) You will find a donkey tied up. 3) The donkey has never been ridden. 4) Untie the donkey and bring it back. 5) If someone asks, "Why are you untying that colt?" tell them, "The Lord needs it."

> **LEADERSHIP TIP #223**
>
> Give specific instructions for the work you delegate to others.

Well, the two men walked into the village, and found the colt tied just like Jesus told them they would. Also, the owner did ask, "Why are you untying that colt?" probably in a gruff and intimidating tone.

Yet, the two disciples were ready. They handled the situation just like Jesus told them to deal with it. They knew, at all times, they were on an assignment. They knew they were representing Jesus. So, to act for Him, they carried out His "to-the-letter instructions"... to the letter.

> What steps will you take to develop job descriptions for the various tasks you can delegate?

247

Riding on a Donkey

JOHN 12:12-19

In Zechariah 9:9, it was prophesied the Messiah would ride into Jerusalem on a donkey. Now, before you get the idea that Jesus was only showing great humility in riding a donkey, He wasn't. Oh, Jesus was the perfect image of humility. And, He was showing humility riding on that animal,

> **LEADERSHIP TIP #224**
>
> Be detailed in carrying out your responsibilities, and train your people to be the same.

just like the prophecy said. But there was more to it than just being humble.

You see, when a king rode a horse, he was showing himself to be a king of battles. He was a warrior. When a king rode a donkey, he was showing himself to be a king of peace. As Jesus was riding the donkey from Bethany on the dirt road leading into Jerusalem, thousands of enthusiastic supporters crowded around Him. It was a new look to the long anticipated Messiah. Everyone had been expecting the Messiah to ride a horse, as the King of Battles. Jesus was riding toward Jerusalem, sending a message, loud and clear, to the religious leaders. He was riding in as the Messiah of Zechariah 9:9, the King of Peace.

> How can you pay more attention to details in carrying out your responsibilities?

TEARS OVER JERUSALEM

LUKE 19:41-44

As Passover pilgrims walked around the last bend in the road, leading to Jerusalem, they could see the grandeur of the famed city. Many of them would even drop to their knees in awe. Especially those who were catching sight of the city for the first time.

LEADERSHIP TIP #225

See the world through the eyes of Jesus.

However, as Jesus rounded that last curve riding on the donkey, seeing the same city as everyone else, tears began to well up in His eyes. Tears of sadness, not of joy. He wasn't looking at the buildings, the glamour, the glitter, and the power. Instead, He saw into the very soul of the city. He could see corruption in the temple, dishonesty in the government, and greed in the hearts of the people.

As other people dropped to their knees in awe of Jerusalem, His heart was breaking. He knew what would happen to the "great" city because of its unbelief. And, it wasn't a pretty picture. To the city, He said, "Your enemies will not leave a single stone in place, because you did not accept your opportunity for salvation."

Jesus was able to see through appearances, into the very heart. How can you more effectively look at every situation through the eyes of Jesus?

249

CURSING A FIG TREE

MARK 11:12-14

It was the next morning, after riding into Jerusalem on a donkey. Jesus and His men were now walking on the road toward Jerusalem. Off in the distance, He spotted a fig tree full of leaves. Since He was hungry, He walked over to pick some of the figs. However, when He started rummaging through the leaves, looking for figs, He saw it was fruitless. No big surprise there. After all, it was too early in the season for the fruit.

> **LEADERSHIP TIP #226**
>
> Commit yourself to a lifestyle consistent with your faith in God.

Surprisingly, Jesus cursed the tree. He stopped it from ever growing figs again. Now, that really wasn't like Jesus, was it? Well, yes it was, if we understand what He was actually doing. You see, Jesus was giving His followers a living illustration of what would soon happen to the Jewish nation.

God raised up the Jewish people to bring His message to the world. The tree and its leaves symbolized Israel's great potential. Yet, like the fig tree, Israel was fruitless. The nation got so wrapped up in itself, its lifestyle didn't measure up to its openly declared faith. That didn't please God.

> What do you need to change to line up your lifestyle with your faith in God?

Cleaning Out the Temple

Mark 11:15-18

Jesus rid the profiteers from the temple twice. The first, at the start of His mission. The second, this time, in what would be the last week of His work on earth. It took place in the huge outer Court of the Gentiles. When this court was built, its intended purpose was for visitors to pray, and pre-

LEADERSHIP TIP #227

See your physical body as the temple of God (1 Cor. 6:19-20). Keep it cleansed for God's use.

pare themselves for worshipping God. However, because of the get-rich schemes of the priests, in cahoots with some merchants, the court had become a pit of worldly values.

Instead of people praying, people were arguing with the animal-sellers, and money-changers. "You're a bunch of bandits," they would yell. "Pay it, or get out of here," a merchant would scream back. This outer court was also used as a short-cut for people walking from the eastern part of Jerusalem to the Mount of Olives. Jesus saw that nothing really had changed from the first time He had cleansed the temple. So, for the second time, He chased the merchants out of the court. This time, He even kept people from using the shortcut.

1. Why did Jesus angrily take action a second time, since the first time didn't change anything?

2. What can you do to keep your body, more effectively, cleansed?

THE PRAYER OF FAITH

MARK 11:20-25

The next day, when Jesus and His men were again walking to Jerusalem, they passed the fig tree Jesus had cursed. The disciples were surprised, yes, even amazed, to see it had totally dried up and died, from its roots to its top. "Look at it," Peter excitedly told Jesus.

> **LEADERSHIP TIP #228**
>
> Expect God to grant your requests if you ask for what Jesus would ask.

It wasn't a surprise for Jesus. He expected it. As they walked by the withered tree, Jesus casually said, "Have faith in God, and you can say to this mountain, 'May you be lifted up and thrown into the sea, and it will happen.' " He then explained they would really have to believe God would do it. Not just give lip service to praying. Jesus knew His four key words to His men were, "Have faith in God." The faith He was talking about implied being totally wrapped up in God's values, and His ways. It meant requesting what Jesus Himself would request in a given situation. It wasn't just a matter of trying to conjure up some gigantic belief. It was believing that God would do what He wanted done.

1. What specific requests, concerning your work and family, would Jesus make?

2. How can you enlist some of your people to pray specifically for things at work?

DEFUSING A CHALLENGE

MARK 11:27-33

Jesus held fast to His Father's ways. He never backed down. However, because of His enormous popularity among the people, His enemies kept trying to discredit Him.

So, after He had cleansed the temple courtyard for the second time, a few priests, elders, and teachers hurried up to Him.

> **LEADERSHIP TIP #229**
>
> Defuse a challenge to your authority by asking questions that will cause the person to think about the real issues.

They demanded, "By what authority are you doing these things?" Just like the first time. Jesus knew they were trying to entrap Him. If He had answered, "By my own authority," the people might have thought of Him as an ego-maniac.

So, Jesus cleverly said, "I'll answer you, if you answer me: "Did John's authority to baptize come from Heaven, or was it merely human?" The committee couldn't answer. If they said, "From Heaven," Jesus would have said, "Then, why didn't you believe him when he pointed to me?" If they had said, "It was merely human," the people would have turned on them, because they revered John. When would the religious leaders learn? They were no match for Jesus. Truth was on His side.

What are three good questions to ask anyone who challenges you for implementing God's values in your work?

Two Sons and a Vineyard

Matthew 21:28-32

Jesus' strategy in combating the stuffy religious institution was to ask penetrating questions. Often He would use a story, to set up the question.

In this episode, He had just told the committee of priests, elders and teachers, who had challenged His authority, that He

> **LEADERSHIP TIP #230**
>
> Keep in mind, in working with your people, that late actions are better than empty promises.

wouldn't answer their question. He followed that up with a story about two sons of a father who owned a vineyard.

One son told his father he would not work in the vineyard, but changed his mind, and did work. The younger son promised his father he would work in the vineyard, but he never showed up. When Jesus asked the religious leaders which son did the will of his father, they correctly answered, "The first."

Then, Jesus lowered the boom. "I tell you the truth," He said, "corrupt tax collectors and prostitutes will get into the Kingdom of God before you do." Jesus identified the committee as the second son. The one who made the promise, but never followed through. While prostitutes and tax-collectors had, at first, rejected God, they changed and went His way.

> What accountability program do you have that helps you see the follow-through of your people?

Killing the Owner's Son

LUKE 20:9-18

Jesus had a way of putting "all the cookies on the bottom shelf." He wanted everyone to grab hold of what He was saying. He liked using short stories rather than giving long, drawn-out academic monologues. And, the people loved His stories. They understood them.

LEADERSHIP TIP #231

Tell stories to illustrate important truths about God and His ways.

Even His enemies were amazed at His teaching.

Now, in this episode, after His confrontation with the religious leaders, Jesus turned to the people and told a story about a vineyard owner. He said the owner sent a servant to collect his share of crops from the tenants, but the tenants killed the servant. The owner sent two more servants, and both of them were brutally attacked. Finally, he sent his own son, and the tenants even killed the son. They were hoping they would eventually, themselves, get ownership of the vineyard. When Jesus' listeners said, "May nothing like that ever happen," He quoted Psalm 118:22. Then, He asked, "What do you think this means, 'The stone the builders rejected has now become the cornerstone.'?"

1. What was Jesus wanting the people to understand with His story?

2. How can you implement stories into your team meetings?

CAESAR AND GOD

MATTHEW 22:15-22

After Jesus had taken the attack to the religious leaders, they counterattacked. Many of the leaders got together to think up a question they could ask Jesus. One that would get Him into trouble, no matter how He answered. Finally, they had one.

LEADERSHIP TIP #232

Give to those who are above you in authority in a way that's pleasing to God.

After flattering Him, they asked, "Is it right to pay taxes to Caesar, or not?" Now, if Jesus replied, "Yes, it is," the people would have turned on Him. Jewish people hated paying taxes to the Roman government that was controlling their land. If Jesus answered, "No, it isn't," He would have had the Roman government coming down on Him.

Either way, He would have lost.

Jesus thoughtfully replied, "Give me a coin." They handed Him one, and He asked, "Whose picture and title are stamped on it?" "Caesar," they replied. "Then," Jesus said, perhaps smiling, "Render to Caesar what is Caesar's, and to God what is God's." They walked away, shaking their head in amazement. So much for their counterattack.

In what way does God work through the authority of those above you?

Eternal Viewpoint

MATTHEW 22:23-33

The politically-motivated Sadducees took up the attack against Jesus after the religious-minded Pharisees walked away, scratching their heads. Now, the Sadducees didn't get along with the Pharisees. The Sadducees only accepted the first five books of

LEADERSHIP TIP #233

Make your decisions based on an eternal viewpoint.

the Scriptures. They didn't believe in any life after the present one was over. Walking up to Jesus with, what they thought was a clever question, they asked whose wife of seven brothers a woman would be in the resurrection. Their intent? They wanted to reduce the concept of the resurrection to silliness.

Jesus must have shook His head a bit. He told them, "Your mistake is that you don't know the Scriptures, and you don't know the power of God." Then, He hit at the heart of their own belief. He quoted Exodus, out of the first five books, to prove the resurrection: "Long after Abraham, Isaac, and Jacob had died, God said, 'I am the God of Abraham, the God of Isaac, and the God of Jacob.' So he is the God of the living, not the dead." The Sadducees ended up with the same blank stares the Pharisees had.

How can fixing your mind on life after this one affect your decisions and actions?

THE GREAT COMMANDMENTS

MARK 12:28-34

One of the Pharisees, an expert in the law, lingered behind. He heard Jesus just get the best of the Sadducees, and he seemed to be impressed with how well Jesus answered all the questions. So, after the Sadducees were shut down, this law expert asked, "Which is the greatest of the commandments?" Now, this wasn't a trick question like the others had been. This man seemed to just want to know Jesus' view.

> **LEADERSHIP TIP #234**
>
> Out of your love for God, love your people the same way you love yourself.

Jesus pondered the question before answering. Then, He merged two well-known, but, separate commands of Scripture, into one. "First," Jesus answered, "love God with all of your heart. Second, love others as you love yourself."

The man replied, "Yes, this is more important than to offer all of the burnt offerings and sacrifices required by the law." When Jesus saw the man was open-minded, He said, "You are not far from the Kingdom of God." Quite a statement coming from an uneducated carpenter to a scholarly religious leader.

> 1. In what ways does God want you to love your people as you love yourself?
>
> 2. How will you express love to your people?

PARADE OF RELIGIOUS LEADERS

MARK 12:38-40

"Beware of these teachers of religious law!" Jesus warned the people in the temple. "For they like to parade around in flowing robes and receive respectful greetings as they walk in the market-places."

LEADERSHIP TIP #235

"Listen" to a person's actions at least as much as you listen to their words.

Religious leaders did like to wear long robes, robes that trailed a bit on the ground as they walked. That was to let people know they were a high-ranking person of leisure. The prideful teachers of the law also loved to be called "Rabbi." It set them off from the "less knowledgeable." In their opinion.

Based on Numbers 15:38, Jewish people wore blue tassels on the hem of their robes to remind them of who God was, and all the great things He had done for them. So, these teachers of the law, no doubt, wore extra large tassels. As if the larger tassels would elevate them in God's sight. The problem was, in spite of the way they paraded around, they were as ruthless as a bandit in terrifying travelers on the road. They used God's laws as a club to clobber the heads of the "common" people.

Jesus saw beyond their robes. He "listened" to their actions.

What steps can you take to become a "listener" of people's actions?

259

A Widow's Two Coins

Mark 12:41-44

The temple complex was a series of courtyards, starting with the huge Court of the Gentiles. All the people were allowed in that one. Next, was the Court of the Women, where only Jewish men and women could enter. After that, the Court of the Israelites, in which only Jewish men could enter, and finally, the Court of the Priests, where the sacrifices were made.

> **LEADERSHIP TIP #236**
>
> Train your people to give all they have to honor God, regardless of how it compares with what others give.

The temple treasury, with its thirteen trumpet-shaped, collection boxes, was in the Court of the Women. That's where Jesus was sitting, watching rich people put in great sums of money. Then, a widow walked up. She paused at the collection box, and felt around in her bag until she found her last two copper coins. That was the bare minimum allowed as an offering. She plunked them in one of the boxes, and walked off. Jesus was impressed. He called over His men. "I tell you the truth," He said, excitedly pointing to her, "this poor widow has given more than all the others. They gave a tiny part of their surplus. She, as poor as she is, gave all she had to live on."

> How can you train your people to give in their work like the widow did with her coins?

A Grain of Wheat

John 12:23-26

Jesus knew and loved the great outdoors. He understood how nature was a colorful panorama of one example after another, each illustrating a great spiritual reality. Jesus often latched onto those real-life illustrations in His teachings.

LEADERSHIP TIP #237

Teach your people that the first step in being maximized by God is dying to themselves.

Now, in this last week, before His crucifixion, He told His followers how a grain of wheat could not be maximized unless it fell into the ground and died. In the seed's death, He said, God would cause that one seed to break down and produce many more seeds. From its death, would come life.

Less would become more.

At no other time was Jesus more aware of His Father's assignment for Him. He had spent four years teaching His followers. Now, it was time for all of the teachings they saw Him model, to be put into one more great act of sacrifice. A sacrifice that would, ultimately, yield its greatest fruit. And, the fruit would be through them. Little did they know how soon it all would be.

What three things can you do to teach your people that dying to themselves will produce the greatest results?

An Overview of the Future

MATTHEW 24

Jesus' heart was heavy as He and His men walked out of the temple complex. They were heading for the Mount of Olives, just across the Valley of Kidron. Then, they turned around to admire all the great temple buildings.

His men were shocked when Jesus told them,

LEADERSHIP TIP #238

Motivate your people by giving them the big picture of what lies ahead, with as many specifics as possible.

"Those buildings will be so completely demolished that not one stone will be left on top of another." When they reached the Mount of Olives, they sat on the hillside overlooking Jerusalem. Then the disciples asked, "When will all this take place? And will there be any sign ahead of time to signal your return, and the end of the world?"

In answering, Jesus used some broad strokes to paint for His men a picture of what the future held. He latched onto the Old Testament concept of the Day of the Lord, a time when God would produce calamities on earth in judgment. It would be a time of unbelievable trouble, brought on by the sinfulness of the world itself. He said the calamities would be like "birth pangs" signaling a new beginning. A new world was coming.

How often will you set aside "big picture" sessions with your people, and what will they contain?

THE FOOLISH VIRGINS

MATTHEW 25:1-13

Still sitting on the hillside to the east of Jerusalem, Jesus told His men a story. He had just painted for them a word picture of what the future would look like. Now, He wanted His men to be ready for His return to earth. So, the Great Story Teller used what happened at most wedding celebrations to get across His point. In Jewish villages, many people waited with the bride until the groom came for her. Then, the two of them, along with all of their well-wishers walked to the ceremony, and on to the week long party.

LEADERSHIP TIP #239

Live expectantly each day, as if it were the one on which Jesus will return.

People were not allowed to be on the streets after dark without a light of some sort. And, because there was no telling at what hour the groom would show up, the people had to have extra oil on hand to keep their lamps burning.

In Jesus' story, the wise young gals had plenty of oil. They were ready. The foolish ladies didn't plan ahead. They ran out of oil. Consequently, they rushed off to get more oil, and they got back too late. Jesus' point? Stay alert for His return, since no one knows exactly when He will be coming. Be ready.

How can you develop an expectancy of Jesus' return each day, when, for all the days of your life, He hasn't returned?

263

A Story About Talents

MATTHEW 25:14-30

Jesus had warned His followers He could return at any time. Now, on the hillside, came another warning. This time, to wisely use the resources God had given His followers before He returned.

LEADERSHIP TIP #240

Teach your people to be faithful in using the resources God has given them, regardless of what He has given others.

He told the story of a man who, before leaving on a journey, gave five talents of money to one servant, two talents to another, and one to a third servant. Why the different amounts? The master knew what each of his servants was capable of doing. So, he gave the amount of money that would be equal to his ability to use it. Very similar to the story He had told earlier about the nobleman and his ten servants.

When the master returned, he called in the three servants for an accounting. The five-talent servant invested his talents wisely, and made an additional five. The two-talent servant made another two. Both of those servants were commended, and greatly rewarded. However, the one-talent servant didn't invest his. He hid it, and the master came down on him…hard. The point? God gives talents to be used wisely, not to sit on.

1. How can you better use all of your own talents?

2. How can you train your people to better use their talents?

NEW CONCEPT OF HELPING

MATTHEW 25:31-46

Helping others. That's what Jesus was all about. His men knew that. Yet, as He sat on the slope with them, overlooking Jerusalem, He was about to surprise them by taking the helping of others to a higher level.

Jesus used the practice of a shepherd separating sheep from goats to give

LEADERSHIP TIP #241

God will hold all people accountable for how they helped, or didn't help, others.

His men a mental image of how He would separate Gentile people when He returned to earth. He would separate, and judge people, based on how they treated other people.

The goats were the people who saw others in need, but did nothing about it. The sheep were the people who looked for ways to help others. Jesus commended those who helped. Then He raised His disciples' eyebrows when He said, "When you did it to one of the least of these, you did it to me." What a concept. Helping others is actually helping Jesus Himself. The bottom line is that, to be truly caught up in Jesus, a person has to be caught up in what He's doing...helping others. If a person isn't helping others, he isn't caught up in Jesus.

1. How is believing in Jesus linked to helping others?

2 What are three specific ways you will train your people to help others?

ONE WAS A TRAITOR

MATTHEW 26:14-16

The religious leaders had a problem in stopping Jesus. He was still just too popular with the people. They didn't dare try to capture Him with so many people around Him all the time. So, anything they would attempt had to be done on the quiet. They couldn't risk an open confrontation. If

LEADERSHIP TIP #242

Keep in mind that even people who seem to be friends can betray you if it is in their best interests.

they did, the people would rebel against them. They couldn't afford that.

Out of nowhere, Judas, one of Jesus' own disciples, gave them their opportunity. It's difficult to get into the mind of Judas to know exactly what he was thinking. There was a fanatical group of Jews in Palestine who wanted to rid their land of the Romans. Judas might have been one of those zealots. Perhaps he was disappointed that Jesus didn't have more of a political bent. Or, maybe he thought the clash between the religious leaders and Jesus would catapult Him into leading the rebellion. The tragedy of Judas is, he failed to see who Jesus really was. Because Judas wanted to change Jesus to meet his own needs, he failed to be caught up in Jesus' plan.

How can you know where your people stand on what you are trying to accomplish?

FLEXIBLE JOB DESCRIPTION

LUKE 22:7-13

The Passover and the Feast of Unleavened Bread were two separate events. However, because the week-long Feast of Unleavened Bread followed immediately on the heals of the Passover, the two events were celebrated as one.

> **LEADERSHIP TIP #243**
>
> Give your people job descriptions that spell out specifics, as well as the opportunity to improvise and bring their own flair to the project.

Notice in this episode how Jesus instructed Peter and John to prepare the meal. First, He gave specific instructions for them to carry out: 1) Enter the city. 2) You'll meet a man coming toward you carrying a water jug. 3) Return with the man to a house. 4) Tell the owner of the house, "The Teacher asks, 'Where is the guest room where I may eat the Passover with my disciples?' " 5) He will show you a large upper room. 6) It will all be furnished.

After telling His two friends those specifics, He said, "Make preparations there." He didn't tell them how to make the preparations. He left that up to them. He would trust them to improvise and get the job done right. By now, after four years with Jesus, even as they improvised, Jesus knew they would put His flavor into everything they did.

> What are the benefits of developing flexible job descriptions for your people?

267

Dirty Feet Washing

John 13:1-15

Jesus and His men walked through the door, and reclined on the benches at the Passover table. It was customary for the lowest-ranking servant to be on hand at a banquet, to wash the feet of all the guests as they entered the room. It was a refreshing act of hospitality.

> **LEADERSHIP TIP #244**
>
> Assume the role of a servant to your people, and look for ways to serve them.

However, for some reason, the servant wasn't present. Now, here's where the disciples could have avoided embarrassment. It was also the custom, when a servant wasn't present, for one of the guests to volunteer to wash the other guests' feet. Interestingly, in this group that was destined to take Jesus' message of love to the world, not one of them volunteered. No one wanted to put their fingers between the grubby toes of their buddies. Even after Jesus told them that serving was greatness. Not one.

So, you can imagine how red-faced they were when Jesus Himself got up from His bench. It was about midway through the meal. He disrobed and wrapped a towel around His waist. Then, on His knees, He shuffled on the floor, washing the dirty feet of each of His men. Feet that still reflected their hearts.

> What are steps you can take to better serve your people?

A Way to Remember

LUKE 22:19-20

A focal point is something tangible that can help you remember something intangible. In eating the Passover meal with His men, Jesus created two focal points. First, at this meal, He likened the eating of bread to His own body.

> **LEADERSHIP TIP #245**
>
> Attach a spiritual reality to different objects, or feelings, to help you remember to focus on God and His ways throughout the day.

No, He wasn't encouraging cannibalism. It was all symbolic. Eating bread represented His body being broken on the cross.

Then, He likened the drinking of the wine to His losing blood on the cross. Bread equaled body; wine equaled blood.

Now, why did He do this? Jesus was a great leader. And, as a great leader, He knew His men. He knew they, like most people, could easily get distracted by the world. Even lose sight of their mission. So, Jesus instructed His followers to, every now and then, eat a meal together that would help them remember what He did for them on the cross.

> 1. What are some natural focal points you use every day?
>
> 2. What focal points can you develop to help you remember, in the middle of a hectic day, God and His ways?

269

THE HEART OF A TRAITOR

JOHN 13:21-30

You have to wonder how long Judas knew he was going to hand Jesus over. What had he been thinking about as he listened to Jesus as they walked the rough, dirt roads, and camped under the stars at night?

LEADERSHIP TIP #246

Periodically, test the loyalty of your people.

What went through Judas's head when Jesus, on His knees in that room, was scrubbing the grime from between his toes, yet not touching the grime in his heart?

Just as Jesus could see into the heart of Peter, and call him the "rock," and just as He could look into the heart of Levi, a grungy tax-collector, and turn him into Matthew -- one of His biographers -- Jesus could also see the evil in Judas's heart.

At the Passover meal, Jesus dipped a piece of bread and handed it to Judas. At that moment, Satan, invisibly, entered into Judas, sending him into action. No one knew what Judas was up to when he hurriedly excused himself, and left the room.

No one, that is, but Jesus.

What can you do, periodically, to both test the loyalty of your people to the mission, as well as strengthen it?

A NEW COMMANDMENT

JOHN 13:34-35

Time for Jesus to be with His men was short. Just a few more hours. So, what did He want to pass on to them? What could He tell them that would be the foundation for everything else He had already taught, and modeled for them?

LEADERSHIP TIP #247

Love other Christians with the same sacrificial love Jesus demonstrated, and it will be appealing to a skeptical world.

Sacrificial love. A committed attitude of love that would put the interests of others ahead of their own. A commitment to love through actions. Yes, to love one another. That's what Jesus wanted to pass on.

Jesus was about to show His followers that love really is action. The kind of love He wanted to pass on was the kind of love John would finally understand. When? As he watched the life drain from his friend. "We know love by this," John later penned in 1 John 3:16, "that Christ died for us. Therefore, we ought to lay down our lives for the brethren." Jesus' last teaching, "love one another," would eventually be grasped.

And, would impact world history.

How can followers of Jesus, in your work, love one another in the same way Jesus does?

Predicting Peter's Denial

John 13:36-38

Just after Jesus commanded His followers to love one another, Peter asked, "Where are you going, Lord?" When Jesus told Peter he wouldn't be able to go with him, Peter boldly claimed, "Lord, why can't I follow you, now? I will lay down my life for you." Jesus knew His friend was sincere when he said he would die for Him.

LEADERSHIP TIP #248

Anticipate what your people will do in stressful situations.

Yet, Jesus also knew what was inside Peter. Yes, He knew what Peter would someday become. He would someday become the "rock" for which Jesus had named him. However, Jesus also knew what Peter presently was. He knew the "rock" might crumble with enough pressure put on him. That's why Jesus told him, "I tell you the truth, before the rooster crows, you will disown me three times."

Three times! How did Jesus know? Sure, with His direct tie-in to His Father, He had an advantage in knowing how His men would react in stressful situations. However, the truth is, because Jesus lives in and through His followers, each follower also has that capacity.

1. What are some of the more stressful situations your people will face?

2. How can you anticipate what your people will do in those situations?

A FUTURE CERTAINTY

JOHN 14:1-3

As weighted down as Jesus was with His torturous death coming up fast, He was just as troubled for His disciples. They were feeling so lonely, even though Jesus was still with them. Why? Because they were anticipating the future without Him.

> **LEADERSHIP TIP #249**
>
> Keep in mind that, one day, you will really be with Jesus and all of His followers...forever.

So, Jesus, in spite of His own anguish in knowing He would be totally separated from His Father on the cross, decided it was the right moment to give His disciples a glimpse of their future.

He started by saying, "Don't let your hearts be troubled..." Wow! Here's a man whose skin was about to be ripped off His back, with His shoulders torn out of their sockets. And, He was telling His men not to be troubled. How was He able to face such a terrible execution with an attitude of caring for others?

Jesus knew where He would be after taking His last breath in His present life. That's the reality He wanted His men to grasp. One day, they all would be together again...forever.

> In the middle of facing a tough problem, how can you put your total attention on your future with Jesus?

273

Jesus' Bold Claim

John 14:4-6

Sometimes you wonder at the things people say. All of Jesus' disciples had spent at least three years with Him, and half of them had spent close to four years. You would have thought the disciples knew Him pretty well.

LEADERSHIP TIP #250

Look for the "teachable moment" when a person appears ready to learn a truth.

So, why, after Jesus said, "You know the way to the place where I'm going," did Thomas say, "Lord, we don't know where you are going, so how can we know the way?"

What a time for Jesus to slap His hand on His forehead in frustration, and say something like, "Oh, come on Thomas. How can you be such a dummy at a time like this?" But, He didn't. Instead, Jesus wisely saw in Thomas a "teachable moment." He answered, "I am the way and the truth and the life. No one comes to the Father except through me."

What an outlandish claim. Unless, of course, He was telling the truth. Some people would say Jesus had such a narrow-minded approach. Well, the truth is narrow-minded.

What are different ways you can sense a "teachable moment" in your people?

JESUS ANSWERS PHILIP

JOHN 14:7-9

The apostle Paul wrote in Romans 1:20 that God's invisible qualities can be seen in His creation. However, it was through Jesus that God revealed Himself in a human being. That amazing reality was something Jesus had hoped His followers would have picked up on. Actually, many of

LEADERSHIP TIP #251

Use what appears to be a foolish statement from someone to communicate an important truth.

them had. But, just like Thomas had missed Jesus' point only seconds earlier, now it was Phillip's turn.

Jesus had just told His men, "If you really knew me, you would know my Father as well. From now on, you do know Him and have seen Him." And, do you know how Philip answered? "Lord, show us the Father, and that will be enough for us."

Philip, who do you think Jesus is? You just flunked the final. Weren't your eyes open when Jesus did all those miraculous things? What's it going to take? But, wait a moment. Jesus seized upon Philip's "foolish" statement. He said, "Anyone who has seen me has seen the Father." Another bold claim. A claim to be etched in His follower's minds.

How can you train your people to use another person's statement to bring that person closer to what they want to accomplish?

The Incredible Promise

John 15:1-10

The room was quiet. One of Jesus' men was no longer with them. And, the eleven had no idea why he wasn't. Jesus knew He Himself was in the midnight hour of His first assignment on earth. Now, with just a short time left, He was about to give His men the most important illustration of

> **LEADERSHIP TIP #252**
>
> Ask the requests of God that Jesus directs you to ask, and you will have them granted.

all. He started out, "I am the vine, you are the branches."

In the next minute, Jesus explained how His Father, the gardener in His illustration, keeps pruning the branches to make the vine more effective. Then, perhaps after a slight pause, Jesus made an incredible promise to His men. A promise that would light up their life with excitement, and expectation.

"If you stay tuned-in to me," He said, "and my words I have taught you remain alive in your hearts and minds, you can ask for anything…yes, anything, and it will be done."

His men couldn't believe their ears. Was Jesus really saying they could experience the same results He did in bringing requests to the Father? That's exactly what He was saying.

How can this promise to you affect your work and the people you lead?

THE GREATEST LOVE

JOHN 15:12-13

Jesus could see His men just wanted to linger more on what it would mean to have their requests granted. But, there was more. So much more He wanted to tell them.

LEADERSHIP TIP #253

Take this love test, every now and then, concerning your family, friends, and all those you lead: "Am I willing to die for this person?"

"I command you now," He said, perhaps in a firmer tone for emphasis, "to love one another. Yes, I want you to love each other with the same love I have for each of you." The men, most likely, nodded. They knew they were to take the love of Jesus, which was God's love, to the world around them.

Suddenly, they stopped bobbing their heads up and down. Now came words they didn't want to hear. "Here's how to measure your love for each other," Jesus continued, reflecting on what He was about to do, "the greatest love is shown when a person lays down his life for his friends."

Reality once again smashed His men in their faces, and stabbed deep into their hearts. They knew the time was coming for their friend. Yet, was Jesus also warning them of something in their own future?

What are ways you can "die," in demonstration of your love for your people without actually physically dying?

BEST FRIENDS

JOHN 15:14-15

Jesus continued to give His men their last-hour instructions, as He reclined on His bench. "You are my friends," He said, Yes, "friend," a word that was a salve to their ears, and, perhaps to their broken hearts. Jesus had often called them His disciples, His learners, His men, His followers. They knew Jesus was *their* friend. And, they knew

> ### LEADERSHIP TIP #254
>
> Start each day knowing you are Jesus' best friend *if* you are committed to obey Him, by having your words, thoughts and actions measure up to His teachings.

He loved them. But, now, hours before His destiny with the cross, He let them know they were *His* friends.

But, not just any old friend. The eleven men, reclining around the table, picked up on the word Jesus used. It was a word in Greek that described the tightest bond of friendship possible. They were His *best* friends. Each of them, His best friend.

Then, perhaps with a nod for emphasis, Jesus explained, "You are my friends *if* you obey me. I no longer call you servants. A servant doesn't know what's really on the mind of his master. But, you, I've told you everything my Father has told me. Everything. Yes, you are my very best friends."

> How does being a best friend of Jesus translate into your friendship with the people you lead?

In the Face of Trouble

John 16:33

With the word "friend" carved into their minds, Jesus went on to explain more of what would happen in the future. He began telling His men things He hadn't told them before. Now, it was time for them to know.

> ## LEADERSHIP TIP #255
>
> Expect trouble on this present earth. Your work is to partner with Jesus in recruiting people to enjoy life on the New Earth. He will see you through.

He told them an angry world would be coming at them. As they will take His message of forgiveness and hope to a dark world, Satan will be on the attack against them. Even to the point of physical persecution. However, in the heat of battle, Jesus let them know the Holy Spirit will be fighting for them. He will be convicting people of their apartness from God, and He will be drawing people to God through Jesus.

Yet, in spite of the truth, many will continue to oppose God. They will even be happy when Jesus' followers are having trouble. But, Jesus said, God will turn their sorrow, in the middle of that trouble, into joy. A joy the world can't explain. "Here on earth," Jesus warned, "you will experience many troubles." Then, in a reassuring tone, He continued, "Take heart, because I have overcome the world."

Why doesn't God just quickly remove all opposition against Him?

Unity Out of Love

John 17:11

Jesus had been having direct eye contact with His men in preparing them for what was ahead. Now, He shifted that eye contact. He looked upward, and started talking directly to His Father.

> **LEADERSHIP TIP #256**
>
> Ask God to unite your people in a bond of unity, out of love.

What an experience for His friends reclining on the benches around the table. They had often heard Jesus pray. But, this time, His talking to God was different. His words were mainly about them. His team. His friends. Yes, His very best friends.

They listened to His every word. But, the words that, most likely, stuck out for them were these: "I am returning to you, Holy Father. Now, I am asking you to care for all those you have given me. Unite them in their hearts and minds, just like you and I are united in our hearts and minds."

United in hearts and minds. The same team of men who, even just several days ago, were fighting over places of honor in God's kingdom. Now, Jesus was asking God to give them a supernatural unity. They understood why. They could see it in Jesus' relationship with His Father. Unity, out of love. That was the only language the entire world would understand.

What is it about unity, out of love, that communicates to the world?

The Let-Go Prayer

MATTHEW 26:36-39

The time for instructing had ended. Jesus got up from His bench, and motioned for His men to follow. He led them out the door, through the city's moon-lit, narrow streets, and out the eastern gate. Then, trekking down through a narrow valley, they crossed a

> **LEADERSHIP TIP #257**
>
> Bring your honest requests to God with a "let go" attitude.

brook. In the light of the full moon, if the men had looked down at the water, flowing under their feet, they would have seen blood mixed in. It was streaming from the slaughter of lambs in the temple. Perhaps Andrew and John would have remembered The Baptist's words, "Behold, the Lamb of God."

The men hiked up the other side of the valley to a grove of olive trees, a grove where they had often retreated for prayer. Jesus told eight of His men to wait at the entrance. He took Peter, James and John deeper inside. After telling them to stay awake, He went about a stone's throw further, sprawled out on the ground in deep anguish, and prayed. "Father," He cried out, "remove this cup, this assignment, from me." Then, perhaps pausing for a deep breath, He added, "Nevertheless, not what I want, but what You want. Let it be."

> How can you train your people to bring their requests to the one above them in a chain-of-command, with a "let go" attitude?

281

SLEEPING FRIENDS

MATTHEW 26:40-41

It had been a long day. Now, it was a long night. The three men knew Jesus wanted them to stay awake and be praying. But, for them, seeing their leader in such torment, and the heaviness of their own eyelids, it was just too much. They fought it, but it was a losing battle.

LEADERSHIP TIP #258

Correct someone who lets you down by: 1) Telling him specifically how he let you down; 2) Encouraging him with specifics on how to do better; and, 3) Communicating that you can understand how it happened.

First, just for a second an eye would start closing. Then a quick shaking of the head. Both eyes were open again. They would look over at Jesus. In the moonlight, they could see sweat glistening on His forehead as He prayed. Another two or three seconds, and both eyes were closing. Then another quick shaking of their heads. Finally, three snoring men. Jesus slowly got to His feet, and walked over to them.

How disappointed He was. Yet, He understood. He bent over and nudged them, sweat dripping from His face. They jerked again when they woke. Their friend's words cut through the stillness, "Couldn't you stay awake and watch with me for one hour? Keep alert and pray. Otherwise, temptation will overpower you. Your spirit is willing, but your body is weak!"

Why is this three step approach so valuable?

The Hour is Here

Matthew 26:42-46

No sooner had Jesus returned to pray again, than His three trusted friends, once more, were sound asleep. They wanted to stay awake. They really did. But, for some reason, they couldn't. Jesus had already awakened them twice. Now, as He was back on the ground praying, He could hear

LEADERSHIP TIP #259

Accept a difficult challenge as God's assignment, and rely on Him to help you do it.

noises from across the valley. He looked up and saw so many people coming. They were hiking over the same trail He and His men had been on, only a little over an hour earlier.

It was a mix of over 600 Roman soldiers, temple guards, and religious leaders. They were heading His way. Now, in the moonlight, Jesus could see Judas leading the mob. He could also see all the swords, spears and clubs they were carrying. No need for those weapons, though. He had already resolved to do what His Father wanted Him to do. Jesus slowly got to His feet, and watched the mob a few seconds longer. Then, He walked over to His sleeping men. Another three nudges. Another three sudden, looking-up moves of their heads. And, four terrifying words from Jesus. "The hour has come."

What are some current difficult things you know are God's assignment for you, and what are some you know are not?

283

MEETING THE SOLDIERS

JOHN 18:4-9

The mob was approaching just as Jesus and His three friends joined up with the eight at the garden entrance. Judas quickly walked up to Jesus, and with a feigned warm embrace, kissed Him on the cheek. The kiss, a cultural sign of friendship.

> **LEADERSHIP TIP #260**
>
> Once you know the difficult assignment is from God, take the initiative in meeting your challenge head on.

Jesus allowed Judas to point Him out to the mob, that He was the one they were sent out to get. Judas did what he agreed to do. Jesus, with eyes that penetrated Judas' soul, said, "You betray the Son of Man with a kiss, Judas?" Judas backed away. He couldn't say a word. Then, Jesus confidently walked up to the lead officer. "Who do you want?" He asked. "Jesus of Nazareth." Jesus could have pointed to Peter and said, "There's the man." And, in the confusion He could have tried to get away. But, He didn't. He simply said, "I'm He."

For some reason, at those words, all of the tough soldiers fell backward on the ground. Another opportunity for escape. Instead, Jesus asked again, this time probably helping the officer to his feet, "Who are you looking for?" "Jesus," came the reply. "I told you, I'm the one. Take me, but let my men go."

What have you learned about Jesus in this episode?

284

PETER TO THE RESCUE

MATTHEW 26:51-54, LUKE 22:51, AND JOHN 18:10-11

Before the soldiers could grab hold of Jesus, Peter swung into action. He pulled a two-edged sword out of its sheath. It was the kind of sword used for fighting.

Now, the fisherman from Galilee was not one to hold back from a brawl. So, with the sword firmly in his grip, he attacked the closest person to Jesus. He was an unfortunate man named Malchus, the servant of the high priest, not an armed soldier. Perhaps that's why Peter went after him. He raised the sword in front of the bewildered servant and brought it down with force. Peter's idea was to split the man's head wide open. However, he missed the center of the head. Instead, Peter cleanly cut off one of Malchus's ears.

LEADERSHIP TIP #261

Don't accept an easy out from doing what you know God has called you to do.

The soldiers couldn't believe what had just happened. One man with a sword against all of them? Jesus quickly put His hand on Peter's sword, and told His friend to sheath it. Then, He turned to Malchus. Jesus put His hand over the gaping wound. As He removed it, the wound was completely healed. No ear, but no wound, either.

From how Jesus dealt with Malchus, how do you think He sees opponents?

Penetrating Questions

John 18:19-24

As Jesus' hands were being tied behind His back, His men were running off. The soldiers led Jesus back to Jerusalem to the place of Annas, a past Jewish high priest.

For the next several minutes, Jesus stood as a criminal in front of the powerful religious leader, and Annas peppered Him with questions. "What have you been teaching your followers?" he harshly demanded. "I have always taught openly," Jesus replied, "and I've been heard by all the people."

> **LEADERSHIP TIP #262**
>
> Ask an "attacker" a penetrating question to get at the truth.

Then Jesus turned the tables on Annas. He asked, him, "Why are you asking me this question? Ask those who heard me." His idea was Annas could then believe others. One of the temple guards, standing next to Jesus, slugged Him in the face. "Is that the way to answer the high priest?" he shouted. The King of Peace, most likely, had to check with his tongue to see if His teeth were still in place. Without cowering, Jesus turned to His attacker. "If I said anything wrong, tell me what it was. If I didn't, why did you hit me?"

No answer from the guard. He just backed off.

What questions would be good to help an opponent see the truth?

Two False Witnesses

MATTHEW 26:59-63

The religious leaders finally had Jesus in captivity, and Caiphas, the current High Priest took over. To make it look to the people that Jesus really was guilty of something, he knew they had to bring at least one "legitimate" charge against Him.

LEADERSHIP TIP #263

Your silence about false accusations can demonstrate to others God's strength in you.

According to the law, they had to have two witnesses in total agreement. Several people agreed to bring charges against Jesus, but their charges didn't make sense. None of the "witnesses" agreed with the others. Finally, members of the council found two men who agreed to the same charge. What a relief. The two men were led to the high priest. Both of them agreed that Jesus had boasted, "I am able to destroy the Temple of God and rebuild it in three days." Well, they were close, but ever so far from the actual truth.

Interestingly, Jesus didn't say a word in His defense. He just stood there, hands tied behind His back, looking at the high priest. And, not uttering even one syllable in His defense. "What do you have to say for yourself," the high priest demanded. Still, nothing from Jesus' mouth.

Why is it not always wise to quickly answer a false charge against you?

287

Peter's Denials

LUKE 22:54-62

If things were going rough on Jesus inside the building, they weren't too easy for Peter outside in the courtyard, either. Out of a loyal friendship, Peter had snuck into the area because his friend, John knew someone on the inside.

LEADERSHIP TIP #264

A loyal friend, in a moment of weakness, can let you down.

Peter was trying to warm his hands by the open fire, and still not be recognized. He cringed when he heard a servant girl standing next to him, call out, probably pointing to him, "This man was with Him." Peter quickly denied her claim. "I don't even know the man," he shot back, clearly irritated. Later, someone said, "Sure, you must be one of them." Peter frantically shook his head in denial. "No, man, I'm not."

About an hour later, another person pointed at Peter, saying, "You must be one of them. You're a Galilean." Peter had enough. Just as Jesus was being led on an upper terrace from one room to another, Peter angrily shot back, "I don't know what you're talking about. Just then, as the sun was rising, and Jesus' eyes on him, a rooster crowed. Suddenly, it hit Peter what he had done. He ran out, tears flooding his eyes.

What steps would you take if a loyal friend let you down?

GIVE US BARABBAS

MATTHEW 27:20-23

The Jewish method of execution was stoning. However, for some reason, perhaps because they hated Him so much, the religious leaders wanted Jesus tortured through the painful crucifixion.

LEADERSHIP TIP #265

"Mob psychology" can keep people from grasping the truth.

So, they took Him to Pilate, the Roman governor. He didn't want anything to do with Jesus. But, he was forced into action when the Jewish leaders told him that Jesus claimed to be a king. Pilate was already in the emperor's doghouse because of many Jewish uprisings. He just couldn't afford another one, and he thought he had a way out.

Every year at Passover, he would release one Jewish prisoner, anyone the crowd wanted. This year, he had in custody one of the worst of all criminals, a man named Barabbas. He was confident the Jewish people would ask for Jesus to be released. Pilate was shocked when, at the urging of the religious leaders, the people called for Barabbas. "What should I do with Jesus?" Pilate shouted back. "Crucify Him," part of the crowd chanted over and over again, at the clever urging of the religious leaders. Soon, the chant was picked up by everyone.

What would you do if your opponents had manipulated your base support against you?

The Scourging

John 19:1

The crowd had just demanded Barabbas to be released. Pilate's wife had sent him a message, telling him not to have anything to do with the man. What should he do?

> ### LEADERSHIP TIP #266
> Physical sacrifice can reveal love.

He slowly acknowledged the crowd's desire with a nod, then ordered Jesus to be "flogged." Now, in the Bible, the same Greek word is used for both the Jewish flogging, and the Roman scourging. The context tells which it is. It does make a difference. The Jewish flogging was done with leather straps, and the flogger could hit the victim no more than 40 times. The Roman scourge, also called a "cat of nine tails," was nine leather straps. Each had lead, or a piece of jagged bone, or metal, tied onto the ends, to dig deep into the victim's back. No limit on hitting.

In Jesus' case, it was a Roman governor giving the order, and Roman soldiers doing the crucifying afterwards. No doubt about it. Jesus was scourged, and it was more than a "punishment." It was a mutilation. His skin was shredded from his back between the 18th and 25th blow. If He received more blows, His flesh on His back would be ripped apart.

> In what ways can you physically sacrifice to reveal your love for specific people in your life, as well as the people you lead?

Pilate's Authority

Matthew 27:27-31 and John 19:1-11

As Jesus was cut down from the scourging post, He slumped into a pool of blood. Then, a few soldiers dragged Him into a room where they stripped Him, and put a purple robe around Him.

LEADERSHIP TIP #267

Fear no man's authority. All authority is either given, or taken away, by God to accomplish His purpose.

One of the soldiers wove a "crown" of long spike-like thorns, and jammed it on Jesus' head, while all the soldiers then crowded around, falling to their knees in mock worship of Him. Finally, they redressed Him, and brought Him to Pilate. Pilate was hoping the people would feel sorry, and want to release Jesus. He was wrong. One of the religious leaders said, "By our law, He must die, because He calls Himself the Son of God."

Suddenly, Pilate knew he was in way over his head. He quickly led Jesus back into his private room, and asked, "Where are you from?" Jesus didn't answer. "Answer me," Pilate demanded. "Don't you realize I have the power to release or crucify you?" Jesus finally opened His mouth. He turned to Pilate and said, "You would have no power over me at all, unless it were given to you from above."

How can being caught up in God's purpose help you deal with unfair authorities?

291

AGONY OF THE CROSS

JOHN 19:16-18

Pilate finally ordered Jesus to be taken away to be crucified. Because of His loss of blood, Jesus struggled to drag His cross through the streets of Jerusalem. However, He did get some help from Simon of Cyrene.

LEADERSHIP TIP #268

Understand God's love for you by the pain Jesus experienced on the cross.

As soon as the weakened Jesus reached the hill outside the city, soldiers ripped off His blood-soaked garments, and threw Him down onto the cross. With Jesus' raw back scraping against the crude timber, a soldier stretched out one of His arms. Then, placing the point of a large spike on Jesus' wrist, the soldier used a mallet to pound it through into the wood. Each blow shattered Jesus' nerves, sending shock waves rippling through His body.

The soldier did the same to the other wrist. Then a spike through both of Jesus' feet, one placed on top of the other, the bottom of His feet facing the cross. Soldiers hoisted up the end of the cross, and pushed it to the recently dug hole, letting it slam to the bottom. As the heavy cross came to a jarring stop, both of Jesus' shoulders dislocated, and His raw back splintered all the more. That was just the beginning.

How does Jesus' pain on the cross equate to God's love for you?

A New Forgiveness

Luke 23:33-34

Because His feet were spiked with His feet flat against the vertical timber, Jesus could not straighten His legs. With His torso leaning forward, pressure mounted against His lungs, making it almost impossible to breathe.

LEADERSHIP TIP #269

As you understand a person's motives for his wrongdoing, forgive him the same way Jesus forgave the soldiers killing Him.

The only way to catch a deeper breath was to lift His torso up. However, because of His dislocated shoulders, He couldn't pull the weight of His body up to relieve pressure on His lungs. He had to push with His legs to lift His torso. Yet, because He couldn't straighten His legs all the way, He could only hold a semi-erect position for a few seconds.

Jesus would sag, again, pulling all the more against the spikes in His wrists. In a minute, or so, as He started to gasp for air, He would repeat the maneuver. Each time, pain ripped through His body. At the foot of the cross, the "couldn't- careless" soldiers rolled dice to see who would get His clothing. As they did, Jesus told His Father, "Forgive them. They don't know what they're doing."

How was Jesus able to forgive the very people who were slowly, and painfully, killing Him?

Resisting Mockery

Luke 23:35-39

The Jewish religious leaders had Jesus right where they wanted Him. Only it was so much better. All eyes were on His humiliated body, maneuvering up and down.

> **LEADERSHIP TIP #270**
>
> Do only what God calls you to do, not what some try to mock you into doing.

"You saved others," they hollered, "let's see if you can save yourself." Then they'd laugh, feeling good about their clever challenge. The Roman soldiers went right along, picking up on the sign Pilate ordered to be nailed on the cross above Jesus: THIS IS THE KING OF THE JEWS. "So, if you are the King of the Jews," a soldier called out, "save yourself." On each side of Jesus was another cross, each holding a criminal. "So, you're the Messiah," one of the criminals scoffed. "Well, go ahead and prove it. Save yourself. And, while you're at it, why don't you save us, too?"

The man who walked the land helping others, the man whose only anger was against the religious leaders who were ripping off the people, that man was being ridiculed by the people he came to save. Yet, instead of proving He could get down, He stayed on the cross.

> Explain why each person was mocking Jesus: religious leader, soldier, and criminal. Try to see Jesus through their eyes.

Promising Paradise

LUKE 23:40-43

After one of the criminals mocked Jesus, the other in a weakened voice, scolded the mocker. "Aren't you afraid of God even when you're dying?" he gasped. "You and I deserve this. But, this man. He hasn't done anything wrong His whole life." Finally a friendly voice. "Jesus, the criminal continued,

LEADERSHIP TIP #271

Regardless of a person's current distance from God, it is never too late, this side of death, to accept what Jesus did for them on the cross.

"remember me when you come into your kingdom."

The man understood Jesus wasn't going to stay dead. After all, the only way for Jesus to be in His Kingdom was to be alive. Jesus might have given a weak smile. "I tell you the truth," He said, struggling to answer between short breaths, "today, you will be with me in Paradise." Now, what "Paradise" did Jesus mean? Earlier in His ministry, Jesus said He would raise His followers up at the last day (John 6:40). So, how could there be a Paradise before that resurrection? Apparently, God has a Paradise for all followers of Jesus to go the split second they breathe their last. Before they get their new, and permanent resurrected body. They will be with Jesus. He promised.

Who do you know, in your world of influence, to whom you will continually be bringing the message of Jesus?

CARING FOR FAMILY

JOHN 19:25-27

Three women, all named Mary, were in that hostile crowd at the foot of the cross. However, not a mocking, or word of ridicule, was coming from their lips. Only silent prayers stirring deep from within their broken hearts.

LEADERSHIP TIP #272

Actively care for the needs of your own family members.

One of those Mary's was Jesus' mother. There, in front of her tear-stained eyes was the "baby" born to her in a smelly Bethlehem barn. She was so young herself, but how she loved Him. And, she knew God had special plans for Him. Yet, was this the plan? Did something go wrong along the way? After all the good her boy had done for so many people. People of all walks of life. Now, like a common criminal, He was staked to a cross.

Jesus looked over at His mother. Standing next to her, He saw His good friend, John, perhaps with a loving arm draped over her shoulders. "Woman," Jesus uttered slowly, "this is your new son." Then, looking directly at John. "This is your mother." Just like always. Jesus was caring for others, without regard to Himself.

1. How will you know what the real needs of each of your family members are?

2. How will you care for those needs?

BROKEN ON THE CROSS

MARK 15:33-35

With each struggling push upward, Jesus let out a loud groan. With each slump downward, an agonizing cry. It had been three terrible hours. Yet, for so many of the religious leaders in the crowd, such a time of pleasure. *Now, let Him prove how mighty He is. Call us out, will you,* so many of them were thinking.

LEADERSHIP TIP #273

Be prepared for loneliness, if necessary, in doing what God has called you to do.

Then, at noon, something happened that silenced even the thoughts of Jesus' enemies. The sun quit shinning. For the next three hours, there was nothing but darkness across the land. Not an eclipse. Eclipses don't last nearly that long. The arrogant Pharisees, who always knew what to think, didn't know what to think. The mighty Roman soldiers, were at a loss for words. It was dark and silent for three solid hours.

Then, the silence was shattered, and every head jerked up. "Why have you forsaken me?" Jesus cried out. "Why?" For His entire ministry, Jesus had sensed the presence of His Father. Now, it was gone. No closeness with His Father. Just empty loneliness. Yes, Jesus felt empty, and all alone.

How might you have experienced a dark loneliness in pursuing something you felt God wanted you to do?

IT IS FINISHED

LUKE 23:44-49, AND JOHN 19:28-30

Jesus struggled for each short breath. A sudden gulp of air. More slow and shallow intakes. No push left in His legs. He was slowly suffocating. His sagging body pulled against the spikes in His wrists. Numbness had swallowed up His pain. In the darkness, a soldier

> **LEADERSHIP TIP #274**
>
> Finish what God calls you to do, and other people will benefit.

dipped a sponge into vinegar and raised it to His lips with a stick. Jesus gasped, and faintly uttered, "It is finished."

His head dropped. No more gasping. No more gulps of air. The religious leaders were silent. The soldiers froze, and wondered. His followers openly sobbed. The man who said, "I came that you might have life, and have it more abundantly," had no more. Religion had killed Jesus.

Suddenly, and forcefully, the earth started to shake. People frantically grabbed for each other, struggling to keep from falling. At the same time, something incredible happened to the curtain in the temple. The one keeping common people from the Most Holy Place, representing the presence of God. It tore. The barrier ripped right down the middle. From top to bottom. No more obstacle to God. A penalty had been paid.

> What significance is there between what happened to Jesus on the cross and what happened to the temple curtain?

NO LEGS BROKEN

JOHN 19:31-37

The Jewish religious leaders rushed to Pilate with an urgent request. It was Passover. Thousands of people would be passing the crucifixion site. If they saw Jesus on the cross, they might rebel.

LEADERSHIP TIP #275

God will not allow to happen what He absolutely does not want to happen.

One problem. Once a person had been put on a cross, he had to die only by crucifixion. So, Pilate sent a group of soldiers to speed up the process. The soldier with a club smashed the shin bones of the first criminal on one side of Jesus. With broken legs he couldn't push up to breathe. Death would come quickly.

He did the same to the other criminal. Next, he raised his club to break Jesus' legs, but he stopped. Jesus was already dead. A soldier with a spear, just to make sure, aimed at Jesus' side, with a trajectory straight to the heart. He forcefully thrust it in. When he pulled it out, blood and water gushed through the opening. Interestingly, it was common to break the bones of crucifixion victims to speed up the process. Yet, in Exodus 12:46, not one bone of a Passover lamb was to be broken.

In Zechariah 12:10, we see that the Messiah would be pierced. How do you explain how God prevented the legs of Jesus to be broken, which was commonly done, but had His body pierced, which was not common?

299

The Final Proof

MATTHEW 27:57-28:4

Pilate gave Joseph, a member of the Sanhedrin, consent to bury the body of Jesus. So, Joseph pulled out the spikes, and the mutilated body slumped over his shoulder. He carried it off to his own nearby burial tomb, and wrapped Jesus' body in linen, mixed with myrrh

> **LEADERSHIP TIP #276**
>
> The platform for victory is often built with the planks of "defeat."

and aloes. That made an encasement that would soon harden. Next, Joseph removed the stake holding back a 2000 pound boulder. It slammed into the trench, sealing off the entrance.

Pilate ordered a cord strung around the boulder, attaching to both sides of the cave with clay. The Roman seal was affixed to the cord and the boulder. Anyone caught tampering with that seal would be executed. Then, it happened. Before sunrise the next day, with Roman soldiers standing guard, the ground shook violently. The soldiers, most likely, seeing an angel toss the boulder to the side, collapsed to the ground, out cold. At the entrance, Jesus came into sight, probably in a garment given to Him by the angel. He walked out of the tomb, and past the unconscious guard. Just like He said He would.

1. Why did Jesus wait until the tomb was sealed and guarded before He rose? And, why is the resurrection called, "The Final Proof?"

2. How have you seen God turn defeats into victories?

Evidence for Thomas

Luke 24:1-12 and John 20:24-29

Several women, after finding the tomb empty, later met Jesus on the road. Excitedly, they raced into Jerusalem as fast as they could to tell the disciples. Rushing through the door, they blurted out "He has risen!"

LEADERSHIP TIP #277

Help a skeptic believe, by presenting evidence.

The disciples didn't believe them. However, Peter and John, threw caution to the wind, and sprinted out to the tomb. They wanted to check it out for themselves. In the tomb, the men saw something that convinced them the women were telling the truth.

Later that night, behind locked doors, Jesus suddenly appeared to the surprised disciples. He was casual with them, even eating a piece of broiled fish. Well, Thomas wasn't with them that night. And, no matter how hard they tried, the men and women couldn't convince him. Eight days later, Thomas was with them. Again, behind locked doors, Jesus, once more, suddenly appeared. He stretched out his hands toward Thomas, and said, "Put your finger here, Thomas. Take a look at my hands. Put your hand here in my side wound." Thomas was overwhelmed with the *living* evidence, and he believed.

1. Why did Jesus still have wounds in His resurrected body?

2. What evidence can you show a skeptic?

301

Peter's New Challenge

JOHN 21:15-17

Several days later, in Galilee, Jesus and His men ate a fish breakfast on the shoreline of the lake. Right after breakfast, Jesus singled Peter out to go for a walk. As the two strolled along the lake, Jesus causally turned, and asked, "Do you love me more than these?"

LEADERSHIP TIP #278

Express confidence in a person who has had a recent failure, by giving a new challenge.

Now, Jesus used the word for love that is a total giving of oneself. However, when Peter replied, "Yes, Lord, you know I love you," he used the word for a close friendship. A second time, Jesus asked, and, a second time Peter replied the same way. Finally, a third time, Jesus used the word Peter was using. Friendship.

Jesus might have been trying to get Peter to establish what loyalty he was going to give Jesus in the years ahead. Would it be a friendship, and a friendship only? Or, would it be the kind of devoted love that would enable Peter to overcome all the obstacles in getting Jesus' message to the world? Each time Peter answered, Jesus gave him the challenge: "Take care of my sheep." A new challenge for a failed person.

Give an example of the kind of challenge you would give a person who has already let you down.

The Great Commission

MATTHEW 28:18-20

Jesus sent word for His eleven disciples to meet Him on a mountain in Galilee. It was time to give them their "marching orders." The day came, and the eleven hiked up the mountainside. Sure enough, there was Jesus walking down the slope toward them. When they

> **LEADERSHIP TIP #279**
>
> Base your purpose statement, on Jesus' Great Commission.

saw Him, some of them had doubt, or wonder, in their mind. Oh, they knew He was there. He was plain enough to see. But, how could He be there? It was beyond their brain power.

Most likely, after a round of embraces, Jesus had them sit down on the slope, sprinkled with spring wildflowers. All eyes were riveted on Him. "My Father," He began, "has given me the authority to give you this command." As the men looked on with anticipation, Jesus continued, "I want you to make followers of all the nations. First, have people take on a new identity with me by baptizing them into the name of the Father, Son and Holy Spirit. Second, teach these new followers everything I have taught you…"

1. How might the multi-colored spring flowers have helped Jesus' followers to grasp what He was telling them to do?

2. How do we get "every follower a leader, and every leader a follower" from this commission?

303

A New Partnership

MATTHEW 28:18-20

Jesus might have paused a few seconds to let His orders sink in. He could see they were chewing it over. Yet, He knew it would be a hard road for them. Satan would be out to beat them everyway he could. Sometimes with outright opposition. Mostly, however, through subtle temptations to get

> **LEADERSHIP TIP #280**
>
> Mentally be aware of the presence of Jesus as you are caught up in His mission.

them off track. Perhaps, as they were mulling over His command, Jesus got to His feet, and walked out in front of them.

That's when He gave them the greatest promise of all. One that would give them the strength to climb the highest mountains, and forge the most turbulent of life's rivers.

"Listen to me very closely," Jesus said, in a reassuring tone. "Pay attention to what I'm about to say. As you carry out my orders, I will be with you always, in every situation, even up to the time of ushering in the new world." That seemed too good to be true. As present as Jesus had been with them for the last four years, He promised to still be with them as they carried out His instructions. They wouldn't be alone. They would be in a new partnership with Him. They could count on it.

> What can you do to be aware of the presence of Jesus?

Keep Looking

Luke 24:50-53 and Acts 1:10-11

A few days later, Jesus and His men were back down in the Jerusalem area. The time had come for Him to physically leave His friends. The good news was, according to God's plan, they would eventually live together with all of Jesus' followers on the New Earth. Never to be apart again.

> **LEADERSHIP TIP #281**
>
> In anticipation of Jesus' return to earth, keep following His orders in everything you do.

Jesus led His men out to Bethany, located at the base of the Mount of Olives, near the Garden of Gethsemane.

Together, they hiked up 830 meters to the rounded top of the hill. Standing at the summit, Jesus turned and said His "until we meet again" goodbyes. Perhaps, He reminded them to take seriously His parable of the talents. Then, before their surprised eyes, He mysteriously began to lift off from the grassy knoll. Their eyes followed Him until He got caught up in a cloud that kept moving further away. Suddenly, two men in white clothes stood with them. "Why are you men from Galilee standing here and looking up into the sky?" one of them asked. "Jesus has been taken to heaven. But he will come back in the same way that you have seen him go."

> How can you, successfully, keep one eye on Jesus' return, and the other on what He has called you to do?

EXTRAS

INTERVIEW WITH JESUS
LEADERSHIP STRATEGIES

DEDICATED TO
LANCE DUNCAN & TOM ANTHONY

This section is in honor of my two sons-in-law. As a guy with a competitive weightlifting background, when I thought about having kids, I naturally thought about having a few junior weightlifters. It really wasn't reasonable for me to keep that dream alive when God gave Peggy and me two beautiful daughters, instead of "no pain, no gain" sons. So, all I could do is hope. I knew the bait was attractive. Little did I realize, what a great catch that "bait" would have. Now, I do have a son. In fact, two of them. And, I couldn't be more proud. I'll tell you why.

In this section, called Extras, we have an Interview With Jesus, designed to help a person connect with God, and a brief section on Leadership Strategies, covering all the tips in this book.

Lance and Tom, I see in both of you a great desire to help other people in your worlds of influence connect with God, through Jesus. Lance, you put it in the motto, and vision of your company. Tom, you constantly are relating to your staff in a way that's attracting them to see God in an attractive way. You both have a great desire to implement God's values and methods in your businesses. And, I really like that. My dream has been fulfilled in the two of you. I do have two sons, who, also, have become my friends. That's "extra" special.

INTERVIEW WITH JESUS

As far as we know, Jesus was never formally interviewed. However, what you are about to read is what could have taken place if reporters had been around. All of Jesus' answers are based on His statements in the Bible.

INTERVIEWER: You've created quite a stir all over the world. What do you want to do?

JESUS: I want to give you life in all of its fullness, a life connected to God, a life that you can only experience through me. (John 10:10)

INTERVIEWER: People have told me I'll be all right with God if I just do enough good works.

JESUS: Ignore those people. They're blind guides trying to lead the blind. So watch out! With them leading, you're both liable to fall into a ditch. (Matthew 15:14)

INTERVIEWER: But why should I listen to you about my relationship with God?

JESUS: Because I don't speak on my own authority. I say only what my Father tells me to say. (John 12:50)

INTERVIEWER: Well, what's His message for me?

JESUS: He wants you to understand that no one can really come to Him without coming through me. (John 14:6) Only I can give you the full and overflowing life He wants you to have - a life full of blessings that will last forever in His presence! (John 10:10)

INTERVIEWER: What you say sounds good. How can I have this life you're talking about?

JESUS: By being born spiritually. (John 3:3) By realizing that you're separated from God because of your sins, and when you accept my payment on the cross that canceled out those sins. (John 3:7-15)

NOTE: Sin is an archery term meaning, "missing the mark of perfection." The sin-mark was the distance from the bulls-eye to where the arrow actually hit. Biblically speaking, sin is simply missing the mark of God's perfection, whether it be in thought, attitude, or action.

INTERVIEWER: What if I don't accept your payment?

JESUS: Then, sadly, you will have your sins separating you from God, and one day, as you step into eternity, you'll have to stand before a perfect God on your own merit. If that's your choice, and I hope it isn't, you'll spend an agonizing eternity in hell apart from Him. (John 8:24)

INTERVIEWER: I'm not too big on that option.

JESUS: Accepting me is not a decision to make without giving it plenty of thought. It means you are committing yourself to follow me, and to rely on everything I tell you. If you make that commitment, I will personally live in you through my Spirit, and I will lead you in the greatest life possible! (Luke 14:27-33 and John 14:15-17)

310

INTERVIEWER: I like what you're saying, but don't I first have to clean up my life? I mean, right now you and I are so different.

JESUS: No, you don't first have to clean up your life. I'll do that for you where there are things that need cleaning up. You see, when you accept me, and allow me to live through you, I'll help you live in harmony with the plan our Father has for you, and I'll always be with you. (Matthew 28:20) But the choice is yours. Where you will spend eternity is at stake, but so is the quality of your life right now. I want you to accept me into your life, and to follow me. Now, I'm asking you, will you do it? It's your choice.

NOTE: Perhaps, in reading this "interview," you have realized you have not yet accepted what Jesus did for you on the cross, and you have not made a commitment to follow Him as a way of life. It that's where you presently are, and should you wish to do so, here is a way you can accept His penalty, and make your commitment right now.

Just as there are physical laws that govern the physical universe, so there are spiritual laws that govern our relationship with God. The following Four Spiritual Laws, written by Dr. Bill Bright, and distributed by Campus Crusade for Christ, International, can help you personally know God.

LAW ONE... God loves you and has a wonderful plan for your life (John 10:10).

LAW TWO... Man is sinful and separated from God; thus, he cannot know and experience God's love and plan for his life (Romans 3:23 and Romans 6:23).

LAW THREE...Jesus Christ is God's only provision for man's sin. Through Him you can know and experience God's love and plan for your life. (2 Corinthians 5:21)

LAW FOUR...You must individually accept Jesus Christ. Then you can know and experience God's love and plan for your life. (John 1:12-13)

Would you like to do that right now? Prayer is simply talking with God. Read the following prayer, and if it represents your heart's desire, then why not make it your own personal invitation to Jesus?

> "Lord Jesus, I am a sinner, and I have missed the mark of God's perfection in my thoughts, words, attitudes, and actions. Because of that, on my own merit, I can't be in His family. Thank You for paying the penalty for my sins on the cross. I accept Your payment, and I ask You to come into my life through Your Spirit, and to make me the person God has designed me to be. I commit myself, through Your power, to follow You as my way of life from here on out, regardless of my circumstances...AMEN!"

As a new follower of Jesus, it's important to get involved in a Bible-teaching church, and to fellowship with other Christians. You can also start getting to know Jesus better by reading the Gospel of John, and continuing using this book. As a follower of Jesus, your top priority is to know Him. Why? Because as you get to know Jesus, you are truly getting to know God. (John 10:30)

How to Develop
Leadership Strategies

This brief index will help you develop strategies you can use, in partnering with Jesus, as you deal with a few specific areas of leadership. The numbers under each situation are Leadership Tip numbers, not page numbers. They're given in the order they appear in the "On the Road" section. So, to get a workable strategy, involving more than one of the tips, you'll need to look through all of those under one situation.

Anger Control - 18, 164

Communicating - 13, 20, 26, 115, 135, 138, 153, 169, 172, 176, 199, 231, 235, 250, 251, 277

Fearful Situations - 117

God's Assignments - 15, 37, 44, 123, 142, 143, 188, 278

Leadership Team Development - 49, 50, 51, 56, 63, 71, 98, 125, 137, 146, 185, 204, 211, 218, 224, 236, 237, 240, 241, 248, 253, 256, 266

Motivating Others - 17, 30, 43, 52, 55, 60, 113, 145, 160, 165, 189, 197, 201, 214, 221, 223, 238, 243, 278